GET VOCAL FOR LOCAL

HOW TO DEVELOP A SUCCESSFUL REGIONAL DIGITAL MARKETING STRATEGY FOR THE INDIAN MARKET

I0479918

ARVIN SUBRAMANIAN

S P O T L I G H T
by **N** notionpress

No. 8, 3rd Cross Street
CIT Colony, Mylapore
Chennai, Tamil Nadu – 600004

First Published by Notion Press 2020
Copyright © Arvin Subramanian 2020
All Rights Reserved.

ISBN 978-1-64951-670-1

CONTENTS

FOREWORD

Google has been saying for the last 4 years that the future of the internet in India is going to be about voice, video and vernacular. If your primary content/social media consumption language is English, you are not part of the Next Billion Users, a specialized growth unit that Google set up globally to make the internet more accessible for non-English consumers. In India, that's a population that is probably 4 times the English-speaking market. Brands today use the internet not only to build equity but increasingly to drive sales.

How many brands communicate in vernacular, the chosen language of non-English speaking audiences? How many brands have a voice strategy? With Jio now emerging as the biggest enabler of the vernacular and voice internet, brands need to really invest in vernacular content. "India 2", as this audience is popularly referred to is not about geography. It's about language. Anyone who is not an English language consumer is technically India 2 consumer, the Next Billion User.

The Hindi internet is already bigger than the English internet and will keep growing by leaps and bounds. So will all major regional languages. Brands have been doing regional language mainline communication for decades now. It's utterly surprising that they haven't yet figured out how to do the same on digital.

Vocal for Local is not just a primer but a really well written guide to building and connecting with vernacular users. Often, the focus is more on creative output than the strategy behind the output. This book focuses on the strategy behind the work a lot. The traditional method of creating content in English or Hindi and then translating it using old school language translators won't work on social media. People speak a different language, their own everyday language and not textbook or scholarly language. Grammar is not sacrosanct anymore. Pop-culture dictates language and slang.

For brands to build a successful vernacular consumer base, they need a sharp vernacular strategy. Vocal for Local aims to help brands do that. If you haven't invested in creative resources who are not just non-Hindi people working in your company or agency but actually live in the regional markets and cities, then you are not doing vernacular right. So much of content is about context. What is happening right now in Chennai for example, what's popular, what's the vibe on the street, how do people think, what they do and what they want can't really be captured by an agency sitting in Bombay or Delhi.

Much like the Hispanic and the Black culture in the US and how companies and agencies have a different strategy, language, tonality, context and content for these demographics, India desperately needs one. Can a

Hindi native understand Tamil culture? Can a Tamilian understand Bengali culture? The answer is obvious. It's a big fat No!

Vocal for Local covers two broad areas – Understanding a regional consumer and Winning over that consumer. The two key first steps in any communication exercise. Of course, there is a lot of granular detail in these sections and the key tenets laid out in this book will act as a guide to create content for any vernacular language in India. Some of the key things that marketers and agencies need to think about when it comes to digital content creation which is increasingly becoming video lead and are also covered in different chapters of this book are as follows:

CONTEXT

What is digital content/digital video? If you take it in the true spirit of things, an digital video is a piece of content created to be used only or primarily for online media. However, we need to dig a little deeper. A pure play digital video has to seamlessly merge into the timeline on social platforms. It needs to have the appearance, tonality and treatment of massively consumed video properties. Cats, Dogs, Bottle flip and other challenges. I am not saying it has to be poorly produced. The opposite in fact. Today we have retina displays, high end headphones and speakers which instantly throw the spotlight on badly produced video content. However, if a brand video looks and seems like it's part of my timeline and doesn't come across as a disruption/ piece of advertising, the chances that I will consume it are infinitely more than otherwise.

CRAFT

Most brand videos come across as cleaned up commercials. Yes, they won't have the product window or the ubiquitous branding but does that make it a true online video? To me, one of the best examples of online video is the stuff that Geico or Skittles create. Made for the web keeping in mind the user behavior on specific platforms. Let's talk about the craft of writing an online video. Pardon me for saying this but most (not all) digital agencies in India don't have the creative chops to craft a really good video. That's because the digital agency business in India is only 10 years old and digital creatives are not trained in video crafting. Mainline agencies on the other hand are masters of the 30 second video and they are instinctive brand thinkers. They are very good with creating a 3 minute or a 6-minute video but most don't know how to really take advantage of a 5 second YouTube pre-roll or create a vertical video for IG Stories.

AUTHENTICITY & CREDIBILITY

So, who is creating cutting edge video content for digital? This role is now being fulfilled by specialists. Smaller, nimbler players staffed by people who understand platforms and also know the craft. Yes, a lot of these guys are ex-agency people. I somehow feel that once you leave the environment of an ad agency, you shed agency/brand centric thinking but retain the craft that you have learnt. Examples are Culture Machine, TVF and AIB. They have adopted a newsroom approach to video creation. They pick up micro moments and create content on the fly in a matter of hours. This takes technology and investment in equipment for sure. But without the newsroom mindset, all the technology in the world will not help you. Increasingly, brands are approaching and willing to pay a premium to these guys to create great video content.

FINANCIALS

Digital videos have far poorer budgets compared to commercials. Yes, the behind the camera talent and the actors are cheaper or not as well-known so it helps cut costs but does that mean the client will accept a second-hand product? No! I hear a lot of clients focusing more on volume production rather than the quality of production. A simple example; you will get a budget of INR 20L easy if you can produce between 6 to 10 films. But not if you produce only two. That's not acceptable. So how do we deal with this?

TECHNOLOGY & LOGISTICS

Production technology has not significantly improved. Neither have the logistics of production. A digital video on an average takes the same amount of crew to produce as does a commercial. So even if you save costs on the talent and some of the equipment, the production crew like assistants, light men, etc., still remain the same in numbers. Yes, they might cost a little less but the numbers still remain the same. So, what's the solution.

CONTENT STRATEGY

While everyone is creating content, no one seems to have a content strategy. Most digital content is nothing but cheaply made TVCs. This will increasingly be questioned. We will see the emergence of content strategy that is aligned to brand strategy and the marketing calendar. We will also see more native video content formats outside of the 16:9 format. More brands will focus on IGTV and emerging platforms like TikTok. This calls into question the ability of existing creative teams to create 'digital content' as opposed to 'digital films'. Will they learn and adapt or will these jobs go to 'content specialists'? As we have seen with social media, if the existing agency can't deliver because they don't understand how to, specialist content writers will start taking over.

Arvin, you have done a really great job writing this book and I can only imagine how much time and effort you must have put into this. I am honored and humbled that you have asked me to write the foreword. This is your first book and this is my first foreword as well. So, in a way, we are both making our debuts together. I wish you great success and I can only hope that this book is just the first of many.

ABOUT PRASHANTH CHALLAPALLI

Prashanth Challapalli is the co-founder and Managing Partner of Gravity Integrated, an integrated business growth solutions company that works with C-Suite clients to help build, sustain and grow profitable businesses. He is a multi-award-winning brand strategist, a very successful P&L leader across two start-ups in the digital communications space and a proven team builder. Prashanth's career spans 22 years across space selling, advertising, entertainment marketing & digital communications.

LinkedIn: http://linkedin.com/in/prashanthchallapalli

Section 1

APPROACHING THE REGIONAL DIGITAL CONSUMER

The first section of this book deals with how a brand should prepare itself before it enters a regional market.

When a digital marketer or brand manager plans to enter a regional market, some of their first questions would be:

1. How do I understand this new market?
2. What are the changes we should be making to the existing strategy to suit the regional market?
3. How do we prepare ourselves for this challenge?
4. How do we make an effective first impression in the new market?
5. How do we get the attention of the regional audience?
6. How do we break the clutter and stand unique in the market?
7. What is the existing market scenario, who is my competitor, and how is their digital presence?
8. Will the audience accept our products and services?
9. How do we effectively communicate about our brand to the regional audience?
10. What is going to be my launch campaign?

The first stage of the process is usually the most critical stage, like a make-or-break moment for a brand manager. Given the busy lifestyle of the users, their limited attention span, and heavy competition, the brand managers have their task cut out to make an effective first impression. If there are any shortcomings, it will be extremely difficult for the brand to spend time, money, and energy to again relaunch their brand in the region. Usually, the taglines and the imagery registered by the brand in their launch campaign go a long way in staying at the top of the mind of the audience.

Therefore, it is very critical to choose the right communication strategy to approach the regional digital audience. Starting from the imagery, the creatives, the taglines, the captions, the color, the mascot, the brand ambassadors, immense care should be taken to project and present the brand in an effective and relevant manner to the audience. This section has six chapters, circling on how a brand manager should plan on approaching the regional consumer.

1.1. ATTENTION

When a brand enters a regional market, the very first objective it faces is to catch the attention of the regional audience. It will be extremely critical for the brand to make a really good first impression on a new audience set. Let's take Netflix for example; being a transnational brand, they took every possible step to make sure they got

Indian users' attention for their first original series 'Sacred Games'. How?

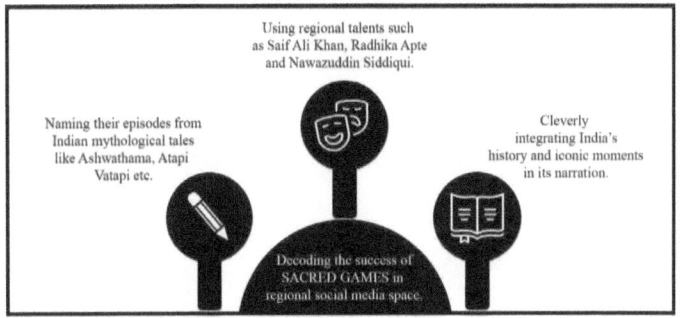

One can infer how a marketer was able to capture the attention of a native audience from the above example. Grab your eyeball with episodic names which sound very familiar (Wow Factor), show the faces of people you are aware of (Imagery), and talk in a language that you understand (Familiarity). With these three steps, the brand now has your attention; it is up to the product to win over the customer, which is the web series in this case. The brand has captured the attention of the audience for the web series in terms of coining the right strategy and making a good first impression.

So, what is the problem that is in front of the brand manager in garnering the attention? The audience set! We are talking about people who are very different from the ones the brand has catered to so far. Right from the language, culture, habits, and taste, the brand manager has to learn the roots of the said region to make a solid first impression with the launch campaign. Also, today's digital audience is fed with innumerable content on the internet. With that kind of clutter, how should a new brand make its mark in a regional market?

We will be looking at answering this question by solving these three questions.

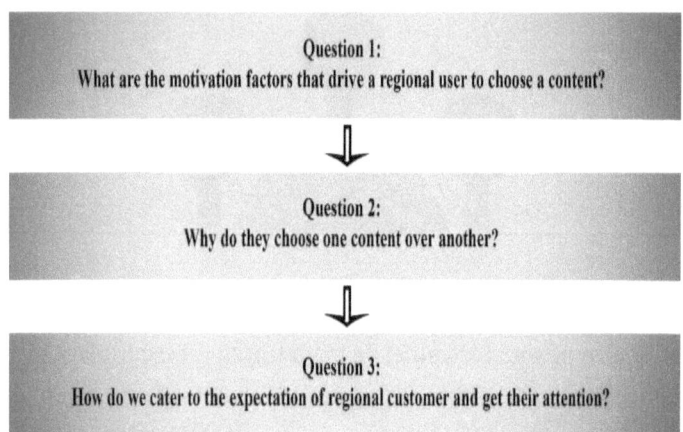

Question 1:
What are the motivation factors that drive a regional user to choose a content?

Question 2:
Why do they choose one content over another?

Question 3:
How do we cater to the expectation of regional customer and get their attention?

(i) The First Question - What?

Have you ever opened the internet on your mobile phone or computer without any purpose and randomly gazed around content? This is a major habit among internet users; in marketing terms, we call it window shopping in the digital era. The majority of the users arrive on the internet without a targeted purpose, only with the expectation of the internet surprising them through either a video, a news article, or a social media post from a friend. This kind of online behavior is even more common in regional markets. Again, the reason is that unlike metropolitan cities, the regional user has limited options to escape from reality.

The internet is the most sought-after option in such conditions. Thus, getting the attention of such a user who is without a purpose and who is filled with various content is a challenge for brand managers. To understand why a regional user picks one content from the various alternatives in front of them, the following motivation factors should be explored in detail. (i) Character (ii) Packaging (iii) Localization (iv) Happenings. These factors will be explored in detail to understand why they impact a regional user's decision to choose one content over another.

(ii) The Second Question - Why?

This part of the chapter is very important, as we dive deep and explore how each of the above-mentioned factors affects a user's decision to consume one content over another. We also examine how a brand manager can use this insight to effectively coin a launch campaign that locks the regional user's attention.

a. **Character** – The first motive we can infer is the user's craving for known imagery. When a user scans the internet for content to consume, the first thing that catches their eye is that of the character that is present in the content. Be it a celebrity, a cartoon character, a model, or an influencer, the face of the content is the first pulling factor. The brand manager has to make a wise choice in choosing the face of the brand, and the content, as this is going to be the launch campaign or the first impression of the brand in the regional market.

It is imperative to have a face that is well known and registered among the regional audience for the content. When a well-known celebrity or figure endorses or features in a content, it becomes easier to catch the attention of a user. In our case, the regional audience is even more likely to consume content that is endorsed by someone who they share a bond with. In regional markets, the bond between an online celebrity and user is very high compared to metropolitan areas. The reason again is that the accessibility to celebrities is far less and hence the virtual bond is higher.

b. **Packaging** – The next thing that catches a user's attention and inspires him/her to consume content is the packaging of the content. The title, thumbnail, caption all add up to the packaging of the content. No matter how delicious the food is, a user's intent to eat it increases depending on how it is presented to him, right? Similarly, no matter how good our content is, to attract a regional consumer on the internet, the content needs to be wrapped with a catchy title that conveys the gist of the video and raises curiosity.

Also, the thumbnail should present the content of the video in a visually appealing fashion for the user to click the video. The thumbnail should just tease the audience with a limited reveal of the visual content and inspire the user to click the video to know more. Social networking sites like Facebook give options to brands to add a little caption along with the content. Such captions should act like a catchy one-liner that catches a user's attention. Smart word plays using catchphrases and punch dialogues which are relevant to the region can be used.

c. **Happenings** – The next big motive for the user is the content itself. Since the user is bombarded with multiple contents on the internet, the retention rate of the content is extremely critical. Under such circumstances, the content should provide some incentive or gratification to the user to gain and keep their attention. For this purpose, the brand manager can employ the two 'Is' of content marketing.

The first 'I' is to invent new information for a user through his content. Who does not like to click and consume brand-new content about a topic that is little known to them? It would be clever of a brand manager to think of launch campaigns that revolve around introducing an unexplored topic of content while launching their brand in the regional market. This kind of strategy would help to add an element of surprise for the audience. For example, your brand is a learning app. You can come up with content that says, "Learn this new method to double up your monthly savings". Now, this kind of new information helps to catch the attention of a regional customer.

The second 'I' is to increment existing information that a user has on a topic. This method can also be used creatively by managers to tap in on topics that are already in the interest areas of the regional customer. After considerable consumer research, once we know and understand users' interest areas, the brand manager can come up with a content strategy that adds to the existing knowledge of the regional user on a specific topic.

Who would not click and consume content on a topic they are interested in and know more about the same? This kind of strategy helps the brand group itself with the regional content pillars better. For example, your brand is a streaming platform. You can come up with content that says, "Watch the unknown side of this celebrity on this platform". Users will be tempted to know more about the unknown side of the celebrity who is popular in their region.

d. **Localization** – One important aspect that brand managers must employ in order to garner attention from regional users is to deploy high-quality localization strategy. Localization does not involve only translations or using local faces in the content. Content should be incorporated with the regional lingo, the catchphrases as well as cultural elements of the region, and preferences in non-verbal communication such as color, design patterns. Local teams and talent must be involved in the brainstorming process and content creation process to understand these regional nuances in terms of the taste of the local region. Only when the content looks and feels relatable to a regional consumer would they be motivated to consume it. We have come to the end of the chapter. Here is the chapter's takeaway - a checklist on how to capture users' attention.

Figure: How to get attention to your content.

1.2. ATTITUDE

Have you ever come across people waiting for new phone release related updates on the Apple Twitter account for hours together?

Have you come across people waiting for Amul to come out with cute little caricatures about day-to-day news and happenings with its mascot, the Amul girl?

Have you come across people sharing and tagging their friends in Paper Boat's creatives that remind them of their childhood memories?

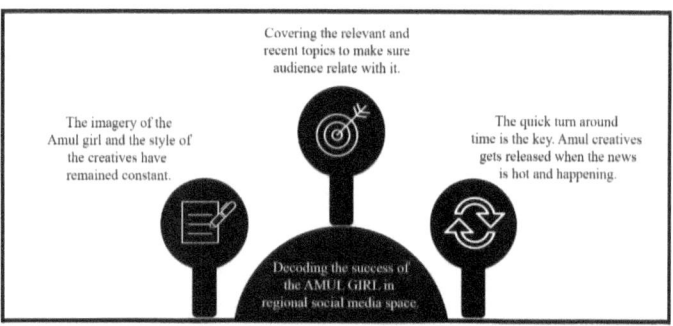

Why do people go the extra mile to connect with these brands and their content?

The reason is the positive attitude the consumers share toward these brands. This attitude is a very tricky subject. It is like a glasshouse built by brands over time by connecting with the audience. Such a positive attitude can work wonders for a brand. It not only makes users celebrate with the brand during happy times but also can propel users to stand by the brand during tough times and even advocate for the brand during tiring times. So, when a brand enters a regional market, it should also look at building a positive customer attitude in digital media because that will be an invaluable asset for a brand when it enters a new market. In this chapter, we will be looking at how brands can do this through a three-step process—the A B C of building a positive consumer attitude.

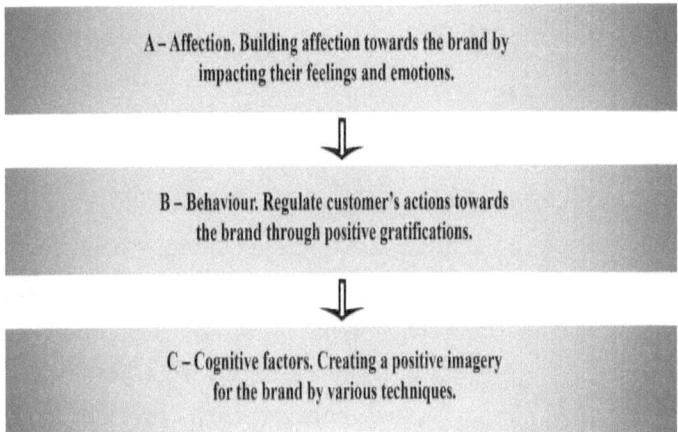

A – Affection. Building affection towards the brand by impacting their feelings and emotions.

B – Behaviour. Regulate customer's actions towards the brand through positive gratifications.

C – Cognitive factors. Creating a positive imagery for the brand by various techniques.

(i) Affection

The first part of bringing an attitudinal change is building virtual customer affection toward the brand. In simple words, winning the love and warmth of the regional consumer. To do that, the brand must touch the consumer by impacting their feelings and emotions. The content strategy must thus not only involve content that promotes the brand and its marketing messages but should also empathize with its customer, communicate, converse, listen, and engage on a day-to-day basis with its customer.

The brand must take extra steps to relate and participate with the regional customer through their various emotions. To start with, wishing them on festivals, asking how their day went, patiently listening to their grievances, offering solutions, and even gratifying them by sending personalized gifts. This kind of personal interaction helps brands build a bond with a customer. This kind of bond is essential when a brand is trying to build a presence in a regional market.

(ii) Behavior

This part of the chapter is very important, as it deals with how brands can activate an intended customer behavioral change. "Call to action" content should be an integral part of a content strategy. What is call to action content? Content that propels users to interact with a brand post in a certain way. Various engagements can start from simply 'Liking' the post, commenting on the post, sharing the post with friends, subscribing to future posts from the brand, tagging friends to the post, sharing customer details to the post, and even purchasing products through the post.

According to the Delhi School of Internet Marketing, more than 90 percent of users who read a post's headline also read the call to action content. Adding call to actions to your Facebook posts can increase the click-through rate by 285 percent. Emails with a single dedicated call to action can increase clicks by 371 percent and sales by 1617 percent. These numbers suggest one thing—if communication is clear toward customers, there will be results in terms of actions.

Actions of the customer can be anything. Regional managers should work out the perfect communication strategy to regulate the customer's behavior toward brand messaging. Consistent positive customer behavioral patterns toward the brand will result in an attitudinal change of customers toward the brand.

(iii) Cognitive Factors

The third step in creating attitudinal change in customers is building positive imagery. This step involves brands creating meaningful customer experiences to create a happy memory or imagery that pops up every single time the customer hears the brand name. How many of you have become a repeated customer of a food delivery service because the brand immediately offered a refund for a faulty delivery? Alternatively, how many of you have stopped ordering food through a delivery service because they did not provide timely corrective actions for a faulty delivery? These faulty deliveries may not have had direct involvement with the brand, but how a brand reacts to such situations impacts the customer's perception of it. These perceptions, in turn, affect the customer's attitude toward the brand.

The same thing applies to digital media. According to a study published in Business Today, over 83 percent of Indian consumers use social media sites to share their customer experiences with brands. Also, 89 percent of Indian customers are willing to spend more with a company if they get good customer service in digital media. This data shows that brands need to focus on delivering positive customer experiences, especially when they are entering a new regional market, where customer relationships are vital. Brand managers need to consistently look out for situations where they can intervene and provide customers with positive, memorable, happy user experiences with the brand's content on social media so that these experiences act as a top of the mind recall value for the brand in the customer's mind.

To sum up, developing a positive customer attitude is imperative for a brand when it is trying to establish a regional presence. This positive attitude leads to customers advocating for the brand consciously or subconsciously to their network, thereby creating a positive word of mouth for the brand. Also, this positive attitude results in the positive engagement of the customer with brand content. This, in turn, results in the retention of the customer, which is essential because, in today's world, the acquisition cost of one regional customer is quite large. Retaining an acquired customer through the development of a positive customer attitude is an important step. The takeaway from the chapter is a checklist of some key points on how to get a positive attitude from customers toward the brand.

Figure: How to get customers' positive attitude towards your brand.

1.3. BELIEF

What do you think the worst fear would be of a manager who is launching his brand in a new regional market? If you ask me, I would say the fear of getting ignored. More than the fear of being accepted, being rejected, the product being used, the product being liked, the product getting positive reviews, and the product being a success or a failure, the biggest fear that would linger in the mind of a brand manager would be 'what if the brand gets ignored or does not even get noticed by the regional audience?' What if they consider the brand to be an outcast to the region?

This is a great fear because once such an image is formed, it would become extremely difficult to win over the hearts of the audience. Always, the launching of a new brand that is unknown to the market is easier than to rebrand a product that was considered to be an outcast to the region by the users. Therefore, it is very essential to get the branding and the imaging right in the first attempt. Starting from the look and feel, the communication of the brand should establish its connection with the region and its aesthetics. This will reiterate to the customers that the brand is making its efforts to localize its offerings to suit the flavor of the region and it should be considered as an alternative option for consumption among other regional competitors. Can digital media be used as an effective platform to reiterate to regional customers that the brand is one among them now?

According to content marketing software Scatter, effective content marketing on the internet helps to improve brand awareness by 70 percent and to engage the newer audience by 65 percent. This data suggests that an effective content strategy can be used to build the desired regional imagery for the brand in the new markets.

In this chapter, we will be looking at the steps a regional brand manager should take to ensure that the brand is recognized by the regional users as one of their own and get the user to consider the brand's products and services for consumption. Important identities of the region such as places, things, personalities should be explored by the brand manager and noted down. These important identities can be used effectively as the brand's regional pillars in content creation. The effective implementation of stitching together the brand's content with these pillars can be done in two stages.

1. Brand Content – Content strategy to sketch relatable content for the brand surrounding the identities of the region.

2. Sorround Content – Develop plans to create affiliate content, surround campaigns, content around content for the brand which are based out of icons and iconic aspects associated with the region.

(i) Brand Content

How often do you switch channels when there is an advertisement break during the TV show that you are watching? Why do you do that despite knowing that your favorite show would return in a matter of a few minutes? The reason is that people know that during the advertisement break, there will only be marketing content on why one should buy a product and how much would it cost them. That is generally the attitude of people toward advertisements. That is also the reason why brands should not only market their products on their social media pages.

Preachy content like why their brand is better and how buying the products will help customers will become aversive to the audience beyond a point. That's why brand managers should mix marketing messages along with organic content on their social media pages to hold their audience's interest. There should be a fine balance between pure marketing posts and content that is engaging. So, how does a brand manager plan this kind of a content strategy that will connect with the regional audience?

Famous internet content marketer Joe Pulizzi suggested a 411 method for brands to follow in their content strategy. The method follows a ratio of 4:1:1—that is, four curated content, one original brand content, and one product promotional content. Following this kind of content strategy will keep users glued to your brand's pages.

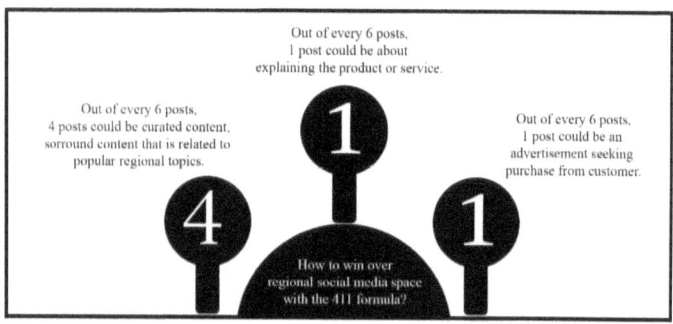

The fundamental aspect of this rule is to keep the audience engaged and connected to your page by posting generic content, curated content, and surround content. And then, seamlessly pass on the brand messages and try to get a purchase. If we bombard only sale messages on the page, the audience does not have a reason to stay connected. Remember, no one will subscribe to a TV channel to watch only ads. The same logic applies here as well.

But how do we make sure the content we share on the page will be apt for the regional audience?

The identification of the iconic aspects of a region is very critical. Be it the language, culture, personalities, lingo, places, food, and attitude of people, these aspects can be the pillars for the manager to create content on. These are the external content pillars of the brand that can be used to curate and share interesting content that will be apt for the regional audience. For example, fish is an iconic aspect of Kolkata City. Rajinikanth is an iconic figure in Tamil Nadu. Iconic regional elements like these can be spun together in the brand's content strategy, like doing a special anthem for Rajinikanth's birthday and using the brand's products and services in a subtle way through the song. The song can connect with the regional audience, and the brand's product messaging can subtly reach out to the masses through this exercise, instead of the monolithic approach of just broadcasting messages about products and its usages.

Brand content connecting such iconic regional elements can be used in social media campaigns to keep the users excited and engaged. At the same time, it will be refreshing for the user to connect with something that they are already aware of and in love with. Also, this kind of strategy helps in reassuring regional users that the brand is well aware of the region and is making significant efforts to localize its communication to match with the regional sensibilities.

(ii) Surround Content

Apart from creating brand content in association with the regional elements, the brand manager should also look at integrating and associating the brand with relevant regional events and happenings; this needs to be done because it may become a little force fit for the brand to create its own content in accordance with the regional icons, even if it has no direct relation to it.

Secondly, it would be better to associate with events and happenings outside its own content to expand its reach in the relevant target audience in the regional market. The first step toward the process is identifying such relevant and key events and happenings in the region from time to time. And once those are identified and listed, the brand manager can look at filtering down the most appropriate and relevant events the brand can associate with.

For example, the event can be the most awaited movie release of a popular actor from the region. The brand can associate as a partner and feature the actor in its product launches, thereby using the thunder of a happening regional event to market its product. In the same way, there may be an activity that an NGO is doing for the people in the region. If there is a temple pooja or activity, the brand can put up their stalls and provide branded pooja hand kits to the devotees, covering a sizable target audience from the region.

Brands can take up stall space in college cultural events from the region and set up product demonstration sessions in colleges. They can also sponsor prize money for the best students and distribute brand merchandise that can add up as a reminder factor later on. The brands can tie-up with an NGO as corporate social responsibility and serve the needy from the region.

Similarly, there may be a content creator who is doing popular regional content. The brand can tie-up with the creator to develop interesting scripts to integrate the brand's products and services in their videos. These are some of the ideas that are listed as examples. Content like these can act as surround digital content, apart from the brand posts. Activities like these can reassure the audience that the brand is being associated with regional activities and happenings, and not just involved in selling their products and services. They can act as some memorable events for the audience, which can help them to get reminded of the brand during crunch purchase decisions as a top of the mind recall value.

So, we have come to the end of the chapter. The takeaway from this chapter is a checklist of the key steps to creating a solid regional brand image.

Figure: How to win your customer's heart.

1.4. PAST EXPERIENCES

One primary activity that a brand manager must conduct before entering a new regional digital market is doing an audit of the region in terms of:

- What are the competitors doing in the space?
- How many followers do they have?
- What are the engagements they are making?
- What are some of the similar products or services in the market?
- Who are the biggest players in the regional digital space?
- What are some of the successful campaigns that were run by competitors in the past?
- What worked for them in those campaigns, and what can we learn from it?
- What are some of the campaigns that did not do well for the competitors, and what can we learn from them?
- What is the cost per acquisition rate in the market? What is the cost per engagement rate in the market?
- Is my competitor doing any paid campaigns?
- Does my competitor have any brand ambassadors for the regional market?

Similarly, many other questions related to the market, the competition, what has happened in the past so far, and what is the present scenario must be jotted down. Based on the same, the appropriate plan for the launch of the brand in the regional market must be worked on. Depending on the past numbers, benchmarks, goals, and timelines can be set and budgets and planning of other resources can be done.

In this chapter, we will be looking at the steps a regional brand manager should take to do a perfect audit of the regional market for the brand. This can be done in two stages.

1. Platform Study – Audit about the various platforms, famous in the region among users and the past numbers about the various campaigns done on the platforms.

2. Competitor Study – Audit on who are the brand's major competitors on the regional market, analyzing their presence and past performances in the digital media

According to Google, India is adding close to 10 million daily active users every month. Nine out of 10 of these new users are exploring the internet in their native language. This data shows the growth of internet penetration and the growth in the regional markets of India. Hence, it's a crucial period for marketers to keep a close eye on the market, developments, and competitor's movements. These audits will give the brand manager a bird's-eye view of the new market and its potential.

(i) Platform Study

To quote media philosopher Marshall McLuhan, "Medium is the message". Half the communication is successful if the correct medium is chosen to transmit a message. When a brand is entering a new regional market, it would have limited resources to explore. At this juncture, it's critical to spend the energy, time, and money on the platforms that would make maximum impact for the brand in the regional market.

It is essential for the manager to pick and choose the battle. Today, with the advent of internet-powered smartphones, there are multiple applications and social media platforms that get popular among users. In this kind of a scenario, a brand manager must choose only the platforms that are extremely relevant for the brand to have a presence with respect to the regional market.

Not every platform will be apt for the brand, and not every platform will be apt for the region or the targeted audience. For example, if your brand deals with serious services like banking, a fun platform like TikTok may not be appropriate. So, based on the demographics of the target audience such as age group, gender, location, income level, etc., the choice of platforms can be made. Audits about the platform in general—How fast is it growing? How famous is it in the region? How many daily active users are there? What is the average time spent by a user on the platform? What is the approximate cost of acquiring a customer? — should be analyzed by the manager.

Also, an audit can be done on various campaigns that have been conducted in the past in these platforms and their success stories.

- Are any other similar products or services present on the platform?
- Is the platform effectively used by any other brand?
- Are there any successful platform case studies present?
- How are brands from other industries using the platform?
- How are brands in other regions using this platform?

The answers to these questions can also be analyzed by the brand managers to make an informed decision about whether the brand should have a regional presence on the platform or not. This way, the brand manager optimizes the efforts and the budgets set aside for digital marketing for regional markets effectively.

(ii)   Competitor Analysis

A solid competitor analysis can act as a definitive yardstick for a brand manager to set quantitative targets for brand growth in the regional market. It can also act as a guiding light for the brand manager to showcase the best practices as well as potential pitfalls that the brand must take into account in the regional market. It is ironic how a competitor can act as the best guiding force for your successful regional digital media launch.

Tools like CrowdTangle, Meltwater, etc. can help brand managers to listen to their competitor's content strategy and analyze what is working for them, what is not working for them, and the reasons behind it.

When it comes to digital media, competitors should not be restricted to our own industry or market. Rather, successful regional campaigns and performances by brands on any social media platform should be noted; how they can be adapted to our sensibilities and requirements can be studied.

Salient features of these success stories can be looked upon and planned to be recreated in our own strategies. For example, Titan used Tamil pride as a great tool to make a mark in Tamil Nadu. Close to the Pongal festival (harvest festival in Tamil Nadu), the brand came up with six new watches featuring salient features of Tamil Nadu such as Kancheepuram sarees, temple architecture, and of course, the Tamil language. It must have been the result of some great regional market research, as Tamilians gift their loved ones with "Pongal Parisu" (Pongal gift) during this festival. Positioning these watches as a great gifting option, showcasing Tamil pride, was a masterstroke by the brand!

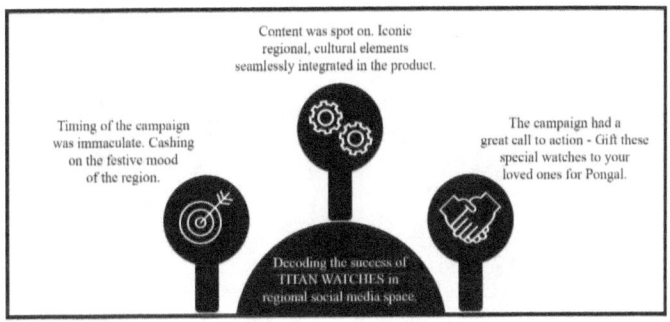

Similarly, disaster campaigns and failures in the regional markets should also be explored and the reasons for the same should be analyzed. This exercise can be done as a brainstorming activity with employees from the region. The case can be given and the reasons for the failure can be asked from them from their own perspectives. This way, a manager can get a 360-degree understanding of failed campaigns so that similar mistakes and pitfalls can be avoided in our campaigns.

This kind of strategy will be very beneficial for brand managers, as they can get a complete overview of what has worked in the region and, more importantly, what has not. A perfect audit of past experiences in the regional digital space is an extremely important step for any brand manager handling the launching of brands in new regional markets. We end with the below takeaway.

Figure: How to do a competitor analysis on digital media.

1.5. SELF-EFFICACY

When a brand enters a new regional market, the important task at hand would be to influence as many users to adopt this new service/product.

How and when would users be positively driven toward using a new service/product?

When they are fairly confident that this product or service would work well for them, they would be effectively able to use the service to the fullest ability. And they would be satisfied with the benefits of the service, for the money they have spent on the same. This feeling of a user of being fairly confident in using a service effectively and making full use of it is called self-efficacy. The self-efficacy of the user plays a significant role in driving their purchase intentions.

How many of you have bought products/accessories that you are not sure of how to use? This kind of phenomenon is even stronger in regional markets, as regional users are fairly cost-conscious compared to users from metropolitan cities. With the advent of the internet, can digital media be used as an effective medium to educate, impart knowledge about the brand's products and services to users, and increase their confidence in using the same?

Well, according to content marketing software Scatter, about 70 percent of users who have access to the internet go online to make informed purchase decisions. About one in every two mobile internet users use both online and offline touchpoints in their purchase journeys. The above data clearly suggests that the internet is increasingly becoming a major source of influence on users' purchase decisions. Therefore, if the internet can be effectively used by marketers to inform regional users about their products and services, it will be instrumental to convince them to consider their brand for adoption.

In this chapter, we will be looking at the steps a regional brand manager should take to ensure the regional consumer is completely confident about using the brand's products and services. There are two such important aspects.

> 1. Usability – Communication strategy to effectively explain how the product and services are useful to the customer.

> 2. Ease of use – Strategy to demonstrate the method to use the products and services to good effect. Explaining to the customer that it is easy and convenient to adopt the new product/service.

(i) Usability

The important step in tasting success in getting users to use your brand's products and services is making your customers understand the usefulness of it. The role digital communication can play to activate it is invaluable. "Epiphany" is a feeling of euphoria when the audience receives your communication the exact way you intended to. This is the end result that a regional manager should look at achieving with every brand communication in the regional market.

The brand has to be crystal-clear with the fact that in a new market, the first impressions they make with their communication will go a long way. Any mistakes would derail the process of convincing the regional audience to use the brand's products or services. So, what are the methods that can be followed to ensure this process?

The first step of this process would be the identification of a USP (unique selling proposition) of the product pertaining to the regional market. This can be found by brainstorming with various functions of the business unit and understanding the real edge your product has over competitors. After finding out the various factors, the ones that can ring a bell with the audience from this region should be circled down.

Say, for example, your product is made with coconut oil, that may be relevant for a market like Kerala. Such regional-market-based USPs must be shortlisted, and market research surveys should be held as a pilot study as to which of these factors would make a difference in influencing purchase decisions.

After the selection of USP, various content plans and strategies on how to effectively communicate the USP to the audience should be planned. The key here is to keep the messaging simple and reduce the noise or potential distortions in messaging. Users have hundreds of contents to consume per day, and just like food, content that is easier to consume is faster to reach the audience.

Some content formats that are very instrumental in this process are explainer videos as well as infographic posters and videos. Content formats like that help brands break the messaging into simpler blocks of information that are easier to be transmitted to the user.

Also, one more method would be to invite a well-known local personality to explain the product's features through a video, using a style that would resonate better with the audience. More than a brand communicating its uses and features, a well-known personality can be a source who can explain the features and the usability of the brand from a user perspective. These are some of the methods managers can use to ensure the usability of their products and services are well communicated to the audience.

(ii) Ease of Use

The next step in getting users to use your brand's products and services is making your customers understand how easy and advantageous it is to use these services. The logic behind this step is to highlight the advantages of your services against your competitors, thereby propelling users to compare the two and make a rational decision.

The idea is to push your brand to an advantageous position during the consideration stage in the customer's mind. 'Zero moment of truth' is the last few seconds the user takes to pick one brand over another. In these last few seconds, the user goes through the points that separate one brand from another, from the top of their mind.

How can brand managers effectively impact this zero moment of truth to win the customer over their competitors? During the first stage, we found out our USP (unique selling propositions); in this step, managers should look at developing POD (point of difference). For example, you are a phone company. Your brand has a local service center in the region, while your competitors have their centers in the nearby city. That can be a great POD in the regional market. This POD can be glorified using effective communication techniques.

Similarly, analyzing with the various functions of the business unit, various points of difference of your brand compared to competitors can be circled down. And the PODs that can be relevant to the region can be explored.

By means of market study using surveys, the POD which can clearly put your brand on top of the competitor in the user's mind can be studied and selected. That POD can be effectively highlighted through campaigns and various content pieces such as infographics and explainer videos. Formats such as having frames of before the product and after the product next to each other can be used to showcase the difference that this brand can do to the user.

For example, the campaign of Lifebuoy, which has the popular punchline "Bunty tera sabun slow hai kya", showcased the point of difference between Lifebuoy and its competitors—that Lifebuoy kills germs faster than other competitors. The effective communication line, the smart punchline, and the visual imagery of comparing two users—one using the product and the other being a non-user—delivered the point home!

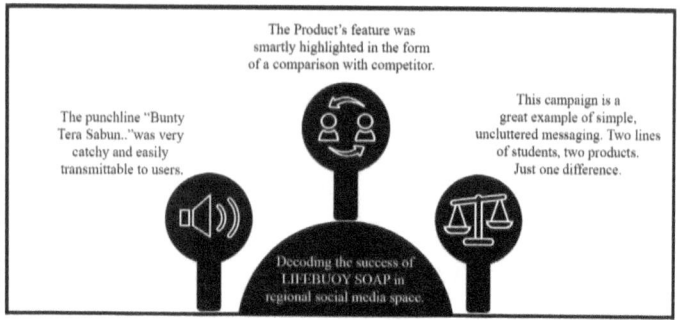

These kinds of strategies can help the brand to push the notion of how easy and advantageous it is to use their brand, therefore helping the customer to make their favorable decision toward the brand, faster and easier.

So, we have come to the end of the chapter. The takeaway from this chapter is a chart highlighting the steps to convince the user to become a customer.

Figure: How to convince the user to become a customer on digital media.

1.6. CONTENT QUALITY

Building a brand's presence on digital media is a tricky job. The major reason is that unlike other platforms, digital media allows a non-personal entity like a brand to have a personality. Social media pages have the ability to like, love, engage, comment, interact, listen, and communicate messages just like a person does. However, the challenge here is as mentioned before—a brand is a non-personal entity.

Does that mean that the way the brand talks, communicates, and engages with a user depends on the manager who handles it?

Does the admin who manages the account determine a brand's presence on digital media. If that is the case, would that mean when the manager in charge of the brand changes, will the personality of the brand also change?

The answer is NO.

Just like how there are brand guidelines set for designs, colors, tonality for offline communications, the characteristics and personality must be crafted for a brand's online presence too. This has to be done to ensure that consistency in brand communication is maintained across platforms and campaigns. Animoto's 2018 State of Social Video Marketer Trends states that 73 percent of online consumers are impacted by a brand's social media presence while making a purchase decision. This data suggests that how a brand positions itself on social media and how it communicates make a great impact on its customers.

When a brand enters a new regional market, it becomes all the more important to define the characteristics, personality, and tonality of the brand on how it is going to operate in the regional market space. Conversational marketing platform Drift's 2019 State of Conversational Marketing report states that one in every four online users conversates with brands on social media. They believe it is a convenient contact method to get their queries answered. Therefore, it can be seen that it is very important for the brand to set its tonality and communication style right for the region so that regional users find the brand relevant and relatable. While defining content strategy for the brand's social media posts, these guidelines will prove useful to draw the various brand pillars and the content associated with each pillar.

In this chapter, we will be looking at how a regional brand manager should devise various execution ideas and brainstorming sessions to freeze the personality of a brand on digital media. There are three such important elements.

1. Hygiene – This is the status quo presence of a brand. How does a brand behave on a normal day, what are the topics will the brand talk about, how will it talk and the tonality in terms of design and word play?

2. Aspiration – What are the short term and long-term goals, that the brand is trying to achieve in regional market and how is it planning to do the same.

3. Target - What are the targets that the brand is setting for itself in a stipulated time period and what does it aspire to become in that time period?

(i) Hygiene

Users receive thousands of communications from various sources every day. We live in the midst of this information overload on social media. The only way your brand communication stands out is when a unique solid online personality is built for the brand. Starting from the background colors, to the fonts, the patterns, the models selected, and the design elements, the design aesthetics of the brand creatives should be in line with the brand's guidelines and also be in sync with the regional sensibilities.

Similarly, the choice of words used in the copy, the tonality, the figure of speech, the style of speech should also be in sync with the brand's personality and match with the taste of the regional market. One easy way to figure out the digital personality of a brand is to compare the brand to a living person.

- What if your brand was a living person?
- How would it behave?
- Which celebrity can you compare your brand to?

Once we figure out the answers to the above questions, we can easily map out the characteristics of the celebrity to that of the brand. Take imaginary situations and figure out how your brand would react. For example, if a user passes a witty comment, will you smile and acknowledge it? Will you ignore the comment? Will you clock the user for making you look small in public, or will you reply with a funnier banter? Which of the above options will you pick?

Now that defines a brand's character. A series of such questions can be formed as a bank, and important stakeholders can sit together and brainstorm and together figure out the brand's online personality and characteristics. Once this is fixed, it becomes easier for the brand manager to set up the narrative in the regional market on what the brand is, how it's positioned, what it stands for, and how the digital journey of the brand is going to be.

(ii) Aspiration

Once the guidelines on how and what the brand is going to communicate have been figured out, the next part of the puzzle is to set directions for growth. Brand managers can set up targets in terms of quantity as well as quality. In terms of quantity, an important metric can be the number of regional followers the brand has at the end of 1 year.

The number of engagements per month, average engagement rate per post, number of views per video, number of user-generated content from campaigns—these are some of the common targets that can be set by brand managers for their regional markets. Similarly, qualitative targets can also be set. For example,

(i) "We have to do a great influencer campaign for Mother's Day."

(ii) "We can do a great meet and greet event with the TikTok users from this region."

(iii) "In this year, we aspire to be known among regional users as a cool and friendly brand."

These deliverables cannot be measured by numbers but are set to set goals, to increment the brand image in the regional markets. Based on the qualitative and quantitative targets, budgets can be devised. The budgets can be optimized to sketch out various content plans and strategies. Content plans can involve answers to questions such as:

(i)   How many posts does the brand plan to post per day?

(ii) What kind of posts? Is it going to be videos, pictures, text?

(iii) At what time are the posts going to be posted?

(iv) How is the budget going to be split up? For influencer campaigns, for advertisements?

(v)   What is going to be the content buckets for the brand posts?

(vi) What is going to be the brand pillars for the content buckets?

Based on the various aspirations of the brand and based on the personality of the brand, the content calendar for the year can be devised by the manager. The content calendar will have the communication routes that a brand can take to post content.

For example, information transfer can be a communication route. This route will give the brand managers direction to post content. Several infographics, videos, etc. can be created to transfer useful information about the brand to the users.

Similarly, other communication routes can be sketched so that brands can use content buckets to plan the posts and achieve the planned targets. This way, through proper planning, the brand managers can achieve the aspired results for the brands in the regional market.

So, we have come to the end of the chapter. The takeaway from this chapter is a checklist of important steps to perform a digital media audit for your brand.

Figure: How to conduct platform/market digital media audit.

WINNING THE REGIONAL DIGITAL CONSUMER - PART 1

In the first six chapters, we went through the best practices and techniques that can be followed to make a solid first impression while approaching a regional consumer on digital media. Moving forward, we will be looking at ways through which we can win them over with our effective content strategies. If we deep dive into understanding the major gratifications that a user expects from internet usage, we find out it is to gain new knowledge about something and seek entertainment to get relief from stress and reality.

As a digital marketer, these are the two routes to a customer's heart. So, when a brand manager plans to enter a new regional market, they should evaluate various content strategies and techniques to offer an increment to the user's existing knowledge and introduce them to new information. Similarly, come out with various content ideas to entertain users with fun content and provide a temporary break from their everyday stress and problems in reality. To sum up, brands must aim at gratifying users by giving them new information and taking away their stress through fun and entertainment.

The second section of this book deals with information gratifications that a brand can provide to a regional customer. Some of the questions answered in this chapter are as follows:

1. How do we understand the regional user's interest areas?

2. How do we get the user to become a regular to our pages?

3. How do we get the user to share our content with their peer group network?

4. How do we get the user to bring his network also to follow our pages?

5. How do we get the user to spend more time in consuming our content?

6. How do we get the user to interact and engage with the content?

7. What are the current popular sources of information for the regional user?

8. How to stay updated with the latest trends and happenings in the regional market?

9. How to recommend relatable and suitable content to a regional user depending on their taste?

10. What is going to be my regional content strategy, and how to compose the content calendar?

It is critical for digital marketers to craft an effective content strategy with content formats that will help brands transfer information to users as well as further distribute it to reach a new audience and establish growth in the market. In this section, there are six chapters to guide brand managers and digital marketers on how to achieve the desired objectives regarding information transfer.

2.1. FOMO

Have you ever wondered about how we spend quite a lot of time on the internet through our phones and computers, with not much intent? We just spend our time gazing through the phone screen, expecting to see some worthy content or update or news on the internet that will keep our mind occupied. This is a very common feature among internet users.

The main factor that motivates us to indulge in such behavior is our fear of missing out on content. The internet is a very instant medium. Breaking news and updates drop in a matter of seconds, and within a matter of time, the topic changes to something else. Hence, as much as the reach is large with internet updates, the shelf life of such updates is very less.

The topics keep changing every minute, and the most wanted, searched about topic suddenly becomes a thing of the past as the internet crowd keeps chasing the other. Given this scenario, internet users keep glued to the platform to stay on top of the tide and be updated on all the new happenings on the internet. They do not want to miss out on any updates on the internet.

Let us look at some fascinating numbers related to phone usage of users. According to Bankmycell's Report, 'The Definitive Guide (2019-20)', an average smartphone user checks their device 47 times a day. 85 percent of users check their phones in the middle of a conversation with their friends, families; 69 percent of users check their phones within 5 minutes of waking up in the morning. 87 percent of users check their phones within one hour of going to sleep. An average user spends 76 minutes per day on the top five social media applications. On average, they perform 2617 clicks, taps, swipes on their phones in a day to check for new content and information.

Online application TrustPulse states that 56 percent of social media users suffer from fear of missing out on something on the internet. They are scared of being left behind in something that the rest of the world is enjoying. That's why users are always glued to their phones to check who is dating who, which social media app is trendy now, which challenge is doing the rounds now, what is the gossip that is going around, etc.

Being on top of all such information gives the user a sense of self attainment, an enlightened level of digital moksha—as the one who knows it all on the internet. This kind of digital behavior is very high in regional markets. Users from tier 2, 3 cities and villages are even more fearful of missing out on these updates, as they have a belief that users in the metropolitan cities are always in the mix of things and have better access to such information. And the internet is their only source to keep track with their counterparts.

In this chapter, we will be looking at various methods through which brand managers can capitalize on this need of the user to build a bond between the regional user and their brands. There is clearly a gap, a need that can be served by the brand, which in turn helps to build a rapport for the brand with the user. There are two methods a manager can employ to serve this regional customer need.

1. Curate - Collect various trending information, updates which can be related to the brand.

2. Broadcast – Develop a follower database of users and broadcast these updates in an interesting format to them.

(i) Content Curation

Have you seen certain brands being extremely active on social media and jumping in with creatives and content for any trending topic, be it any new features or hashtags or viral videos? How is it possible for such brands to immediately spot a trend, think of brand content that can be associated with the trend, immediately create and post the content before the trend goes off the spotlight? Brand managers should note that these brands are run by social media managers, at the end of the day, who have their personal social media presence, with which they follow such trends. They observe their friends' network reacting and sharing such viral content, and early spotting of such trends helps them to be on top of the game.

So, the lesson for the brand managers from here is that when the brand enters a regional market, it becomes imperative for the managers to follow important celebrities, meme pages, influencers, accounts, hashtags pertaining to that region; these are instrumental in creating such trends and updates that become viral. These accounts will serve two things for the brand manager. One, you will get to know your region better; and second, when you spot a trend early, you can immediately cash in on it and create brand content in that format, thereby winning the attention of the regional consumer before anyone. Just being proactive and hungry for content on social media can help brand managers to create an effective and creative content strategy for the brands in the regional market. So, the next time something interesting props up in the trending space, regional customers will subscribe and look forward to seeing how this brand is going to create content on it. The next step would also be pro creating such trends, which other pages and brands can catch up on.

Vicks India uses "kich kich" as a comical villain in its topical creatives. Just like how Amul uses Amul girl in a positive way in its topical caricatures, Vicks India uses topical events and activities to show how Vicks keeps the kich kich away. For example, when Rohit Sharma won a game by hitting sixes in a Super Over, Vicks immediately released a creative of Rohit hitting kich kich out of the park. They smartly replaced the cricket ball with a Vicks tablet. Similarly, when Dabangg 3 released, they showed a caricature of super cop Salman chasing down kich kich. They replaced the headlight of his bike with a Vicks tablet showing the light for the chase. These are creative ways to stay in the regional trend, as well as promote your product in a fun way.

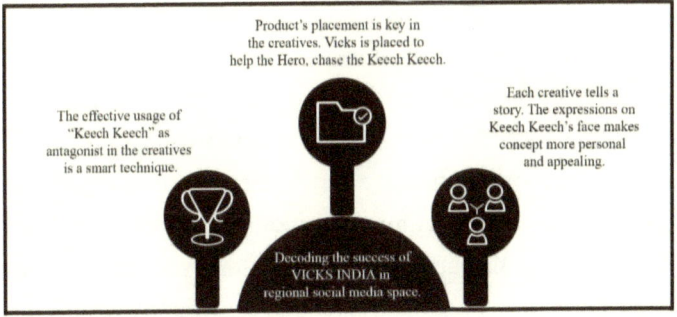

Product's placement is key in the creatives. Vicks is placed to help the Hero, chase the Keech Keech.

The effective usage of "Keech Keech" as antagonist in the creatives is a smart technique.

Each creative tells a story. The expressions on Keech Keech's face makes concept more personal and appealing.

Decoding the success of VICKS INDIA in regional social media space.

That is the kind of awareness and hunger a brand manager should show in the regional space. They must be quick on their feet to sense any opportunities where they can tap in and capitalize with effective content for their brands in the early stage itself so that the user gets to know about the trending topic from the brand's pages.

(ii) Broadcast Network

One part of solving the problem is curating content by following trends and creating interesting content. The second and more important part is developing a network that wants to be receiving such content consistently. Today, various social media platforms are available for a brand to make its presence. Apart from platforms like Facebook, Twitter, Instagram, YouTube, WhatsApp, there are also new-age platforms that are built for regional users specifically such as Helo, ShareChat, Likee, etc. that have interfaces in regional languages and focus on sharing region-specific updates. For instance, apps such as ShareChat, Helo, and TikTok have 5.8 million, 16 million, and 44.57 million daily active users respectively across various Indian regional languages.

Hence, the first step a brand manager should take in creating a powerful broadcast network is to analyze which are the platforms that are most relevant to the selected region. What is the number of monthly active users from the region in the application? How many hours per day does the average regional user spend on the application? For what purpose is the app being used by the user? An app like TikTok is used to create videos, while an app like NewsDog is to read regional news. So, the brand manager must investigate the current scenario in terms of the platform-user relationship.

After such an investigation, the various platforms that the brand wishes to make its presence on need to be finalized, and the priority of each of the platforms needs to be created. Based on the same, the content strategy must be devised for each platform for the brand. Say, for example, WhatsApp is an important platform in the region the brand looks to have a presence on. So, the brand manager should be working on the various logistics of setting up the presence of the brand on the WhatsApp platform.

The various aspects of how the broadcast list is going to be formed should be explored by the manager. How is the audience going to be sourced? Will the group link be shared and the audience opts to join the group, or is the audience added automatically through third-party tools? If there are certain limitations like only certain numbers of users can be formed as WhatsApp broadcast lists, how many such lists should be formed, and how can the lists be segregated—

based on the towns, gender-based, age-based, or product-based?

And once such lists are created, the content that can be pushed through them should be decided based on the audience in the list. These are all vital questions that need to be answered by the manager. Similarly, for each platform, a specific strategy should be created. Based on the platforms' infrastructure, features, and the audience present on such platforms, the content strategy should be formulated to effectively disseminate the content that has been curated based on regional trends.

At the end of the day, regional users are longing for consistent, interesting, trending content. If a brand manager can formulate an effective way to source such trending content and transfer it successfully to the audience who are waiting for it, the brand can build a strong rapport with the regional audience.

So, we have come to the end of the chapter. The takeaway from this chapter is an easy to remember checklist on how to serve the user's fear of missing out on information.

Figure: How to deal with the user's fear of missing out. (FOMO)

2.2. SOCIAL INTERACTIONS

With the advent of the internet, we are all connected to each other now more than ever. Internet penetration is growing rapidly and is reaching every nook and corner of the country. Tier 2, 3 cities, towns, and villages are spending more time on the internet, as they have just opened their windows to the world of the internet.

According to the Internet and Mobile Association of India (IAMAI), the number of rural internet users (227 million) is higher in India, compared to internet users in cities (205 million). This statistic speaks volumes of the potential of regional digital media usage and the number of social media interactions between users.

Keeping this situation in mind, we can gauge the impact of social media interactions of a user on their consumption behavior. Now, the user's peer group is just one WhatsApp message away. For example, on 2020 News Year's Eve, 20 billion messages were sent by Indian users in one night. In 2017, WhatsApp had announced India as its largest market, with Indian users making 50 million minutes of video calls on WhatsApp per day.

With this kind of data, we can safely assume the elevated level of social interactions due to social media platforms and their impact on a user's day-to-day activities. The brand managers can also realize that these social media conversations and opinions of one user can have a definitive influence on other users' actions related to content consumption and product purchasing decisions.

In regional markets specifically, opinions of the peer group are valued highly, due to the closely-knit societal structure, unlike the highly fragmented ones in metropolitan cities, where our busy lives don't allow us to even greet our neighbors.

In this chapter, we will be looking at the aspects a regional brand manager should look into for capitalizing on the impact of social interactions to influence a user's consumption decisions.

1. Shout-out – Getting the word out about brand messages through influencers, users to their network.

2. Word of Mouth (WOM) - Managing the positive image of the brand through PR activities and online reputation management.

(i) Shout-out

In the theory of diffusion, there are five types of consumers who adapt to new ideas. Innovators, early adopters, early majority, late majority, and laggards. Innovators are the first ones who are open to trying out a new service or a new innovation that is introduced. They are generally the most active ones in a group, the ones who are willing to take the first step. Because they are the first ones to try a service, they more often than not are the best ones to guide and advice their network on the new services that are available in the market.

In marketing terms, they can be called as the loudspeakers of the gang. It is these individuals who are critical to a brand when they enter a new regional market. They need to identify these innovators, the users who are more likely to adopt a new brand's services. This can be done through market research and using social media listening tools.

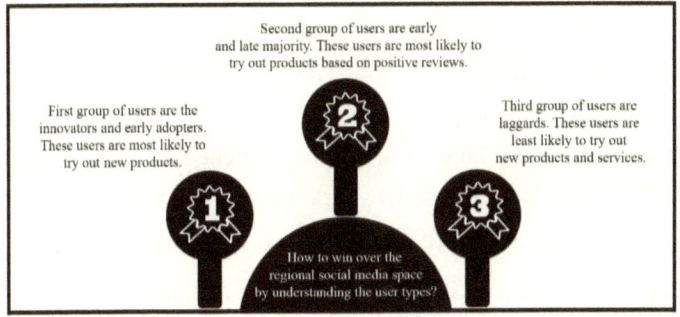

Some common characteristics of these innovators are: They engage regularly with social media updates and posts. They are vocal about their opinions on social media. They blog or document their product experiences through articles or videos. They tag their friends in page posts and ask them to check it out. Their posts and opinions evoke high interactions and engagements. They have a high number of friends, followers, and engagements on social media. These kinds of users are generally influential among their peer group.

This kind of influencers can be used by the brands to shout-out about the brand's messages to their peer groups. Since they are most likely to try out a new service, they can be invited by the brand to try out their services in the form of meet and greet events, red carpet events, trade show events. They can be used to shout-out the arrival of the brand's services in the regional markets in the form of social media posts and stories.

For example, when Maggi introduced four 'Hot Heads' spicy flavors of Maggi, they invited popular comedians like Kunal R, Aditi M, etc. to try out the flavors. They also provided sugar, hand fans, towels, water, etc. to assist them while they tried out the four spicy flavors of Maggi. They recorded their experiences and product flavor reviews as a fun video. This campaign is a great example of how influencers can be used by brands to communicate such product messages with clarity to their followers.

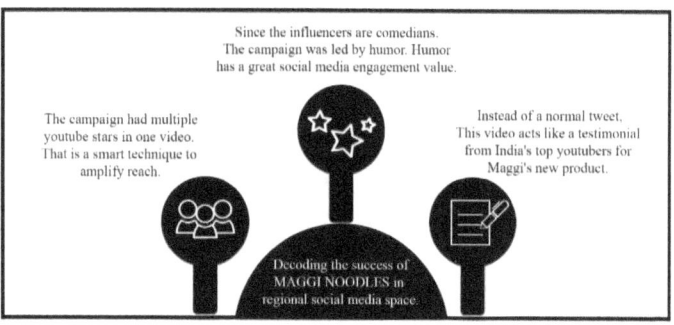

More than advertisements and celebrity endorsements, such shout-outs by these influencers create a massive impact among the peer group, as these shout-outs are not advertisements but a personal endorsement. These shout-out messages turn out as a conversation starter among their network about the brand and its services, and people start talking about the same. Such influencers can also be involved in more campaigns where brands can build relationships and rapports with them through recurring conversations on new services and offerings.

However, influencer marketing needs to be treaded on a tight line. The brands should not overstep in these campaigns to control the freedom of expression of such influencers, as they may end up in counter-effective results. The art of maintaining relationships with influencers through passive gratifications and active involvement with them through recurring conversations is essential for brands to grow in regional markets.

(ii) Word of Mouth (WOM)

Once the shout-out is created, the brand has reached out to the innovators and early adopters of services according to the theory of diffusion. The next part of the process is attracting the next set of consumers: early and late majority. These consumers are not as adventurous as the innovators. They do not easily make the first move toward a service with the intent of trying out a new service and experiment. They are the users who are more conservative. They check 100s of user reviews and read feedbacks and get advice before making a purchase decision.

So, what strategy should a brand manager make to attract this set of consumers? The solution lies in making sure there is a positive word of mouth in the regional digital media space for the brands. Apart from providing good services, the brand must be involved in effective social media listening and actively cater to customers' queries and problems. Brand managers must be aware of each and every message that goes on the digital media about the brand.

They must activate tracking tools in digital media for this purpose. Hashtags, keywords related to the brand and its services must be tracked. Positive and negative comments, reviews, feedbacks should be constantly noted. Steps must be taken to amplify positive reviews.

This can be done by contacting the reviewer and having personal conversations on what aspects they liked. Their testimonies can be highlighted in the form of videos and comments and can be carried out on the brand's official pages. The reviewer can also be gratified with brand merchandise or gifts for their kind gestures.

Similarly, steps should be taken to mitigate the damages caused by negative reviews. The reviewers should be reached out to in order to understand their problems and queries. Additional steps must be taken to make their experiences better so that the reviews are altered or modified with a follow-up or a new review.

For example, when Maggi faced some flak while complaints about its food quality were questioned on digital media, they came up with an explainer video where two food bloggers—Rocky and Mayur—were taken to the factory, where they inspected and interacted with workers to check how Maggi is getting produced and quality tested. This video of two commoners, checking the quality of Maggi themselves, made sure that all doubts and myths which prevailed in users' minds were erased.

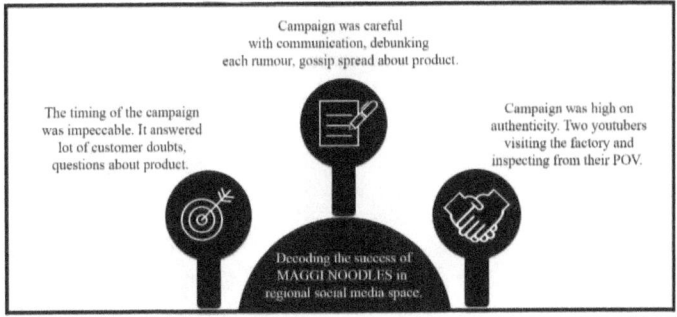

Also, the brand must keep a lookout for such reviews for their competitor brands, to learn from their competitor's strengths and weaknesses. These kinds of reviews help create word of mouth for the brand in the digital media space. These are the materials that will end up deciding whether the customers adopt the brand's services or not. The feedback, conversations, and reviews done by other users with respect to the brand's services will have a significant impact on the purchasing decisions of the prospective customers.

We end the chapter with the below takeaway—a chart highlighting the key steps to manage the social interactions about the brand on digital media.

Figure: How to manage social interactions about the brand on digital media.

2.3. SHARING, FORWARDING CULTURE

Regional marketing often deals with efforts from marketers to reach out to users from tier 2, tier 3 cities, towns, and villages. It is rather a tough nut to crack, considering the non-uniformity in the internet infrastructure such as internet speeds, connectivity in these areas, and the adoption of technology among people.

It is ideal to understand the online behavior of the audience in detail to crack the perfect content and digital marketing strategy for these markets. In this chapter, we will be deep diving into these aspects.

In this chapter, we will be looking at answering three important questions.

1. What is that one common online behavior of audience in regional markets, we can tap in?

⇩

2. Why do they behave in that particular manner?

⇩

3. How do we capitalize on the same and devise appropriate strategy?

(i) The First Question – What?

Have you ever been in WhatsApp groups where you have been bombarded with forwarded messages from your family and friends? Starting from the customary good morning messages, the memes, the viral videos, the ice bucket challenges, to the breaking news clippings, forward messages are a thriving ecosystem. This particular culture is even more prevalent in tier 2, tier 3 cities, towns, and villages. The main reason for this is there are not many outlets or means of exposure for them like malls, cinema theaters, or pubs that are available aplenty to those in tier 1, metropolitan cities.

Today, with the evolution of social networks like Facebook Messenger and WhatsApp groups, a user is connected to his peer group much better than he ever was. Therefore, these networks have evolved to become an ecosystem of entertainment as well as an information-sharing platform, where users keep sharing text, audio, video messages to keep themselves and their group engaged.

(ii) The Second Question – Why?

This part of the chapter is very important, as the answer to this second question holds the key to solving the bigger puzzle. Only when we know why a user behaves in a certain way, we can devise a brand strategy to capitalize on that user behavior. There are three major motives behind a user's sharing, forwarding behavior.

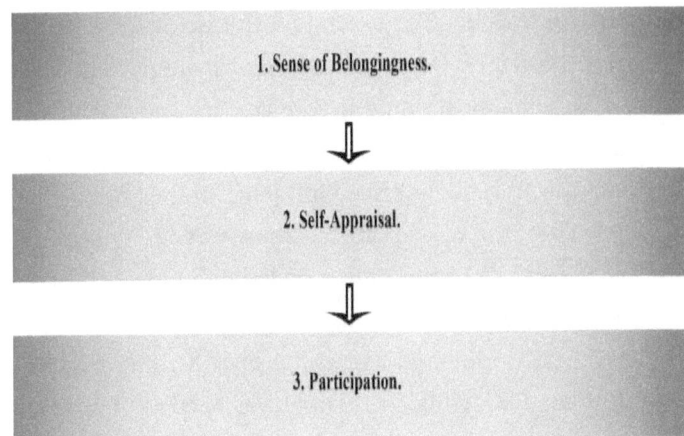

1. Sense of Belongingness.

2. Self-Appraisal.

3. Participation.

Now, let's deep dive into understanding each of these motives.

a. **Sense of Belongingness** – The first motive we can infer is the user's need for belongingness. We can attribute all our customary messages such as good morning messages with a flower image, festival forwards such as the glorious gifs to wish 'Happy Diwali', and sending each other throwback photos from the past and childhood photos. This is a very personal and critical need of a user to reassure themselves that they belong to their peer group and they care for each other.

    This is a virtual way of marking attendance, of shouting out loud to their group that they are pretty much out there and that they care for each other. Especially in the rural parts of the country, this sense of belonging to a family or a friend group is very strong. The ethos and the values in the rural parts of India are very high and that reflects in the amount of participation (forward messages) among the rural audience in WhatsApp groups.

b. **Self-Appraisal** – The second motive we can infer is the user's need for self-appraisal. By sharing important news items or the most trending comical video or sharing the hottest gossip about a celebrity in the group, the user attempts to get a perceived influence in the group.

    The user desires to be known as an important, vital member of the group, contributing such sought-after information to the group. To cater to this need of the user, the brands can come up with infotainment content. Packaging interesting yet lesser known/seen content associated with the brand in the form of videos and graphics can be one way of attending to this need.

    The prominence of these WhatsApp "Information Broadcasters" is very high in tier 2, 3 cities, towns, and villages. The reason again is the non-uniformity of distribution in terms of technology or media outreach. In such cases, personal outreach and such WhatsApp forward messages become the biggest source of information. And the user who shares such information receives a glaring influence among the group members.

c. **Participation** – The third motive is participation; this is the user's need for contributing, participating, and creating content which they forward to their peer group as their achievement. We can attribute the sharing of various song recordings, dance videos, TikTok videos, Dubsmash videos, etc. to this aspect.

    The huge growth of user-generated content among regional users can be attributed to the absence of platforms for these users to showcase their skills. With WhatsApp groups, users forward these videos to get constant validation and approval from their peer group of their skills.

Users in metropolitan cities have various avenues to showcase their dance, music, and acting skills. In contrast, the rural users, who are as talented as their city counterparts, did not have access to such platforms. With the advent of apps such as TikTok, Smule, and Dubsmash, the regional audience has got a window to show the world what they are capable of.

(iii)   The Third Question – How?

We come to the conclusion segment of this chapter, the takeaway. Now, we know about the sharing, forwarding behavior of the regional audience and the motivation factors behind it. The important question is – how can a brand manager capitalize on it and reach their desired brand message to that audience? We present four points that can act as a bucket list to check and use as a guideline.

The sharing and forwarding behavior of regional users is a valuable area that can be capitalized by marketers. This is a method to reach out your brand's messages to the regional user on top of his hand in the form of a forward message. To effectively capitalize the same, the brand manager needs to cater to the three major motivations/needs of the user: to feel belonged, to feel highly valued, and to effectively participate.

In short, the content should be localized, the content should be informative, the content should have a connection with the user and should gratify the user in one way or another. All in all, a sound content strategy can help a regional marketer tap into this unique behavioral aspect of a regional customer and win his heart over.

The takeaway from the chapter is these key points that need to be incorporated into the brand strategy to get users to share your content.

Figure: How to get users to share your digital content.

2.4. RELATABLE CONTENT

Today, with the era of globalization, we see that brands, services, products are pan-country and even transnational in nature. This phenomenon got accelerated with the advent of the internet. With the internet, you can access content and services from any part of the world. The internet enhances accessibility to services in astronomic proportions. This is the reason we see the evolution of multinational brands.

Starting from listening to foreign music content, watching movies, web series from different countries, sporting merchandise, or buying accessories from foreign brands—they have all become so common. Netflix, for instance, has over 100 million subscribers for its service from outside its country of origin. Also, a lot of these global brands have started opening their outlets in India. However, the success of these brands in regional markets, especially in tier 2, 3 cities, towns, and villages, would rely heavily on how they localize their services.

Shutterstock states that 80 percent of customers are more likely to do business with a company that provides a personalized experience that is customized based on the user's location. Localization helps users relate to content far better. Localization does not start and end with just translating the content to the regional languages. It goes to deeper connections that a user has with the content—whether or not the user relates to the content, as it belongs to their own.

In this chapter, we will be looking at the various strategies and techniques a brand manager should employ to effectively localize content to suit the taste of the regional audience and win their approval. There are two such important uses of social interactions.

1. Internal – Setting up internal teams, resources, sources and processes to get intelligence on localizing content according to regional sensibilities.

2. External – Getting insights about the particular region and it's characteristics from various sources outside the company, such as customers, agencies, influencers, and experts through recurring discussions.

(i) Internal

One of the first things brand managers must focus on before taking their brands to regional markets is to build a good team. Hiring the right people is an extremely important process. The brands may have been in the industry for quite a long time; however, since they are entering a new regional market, it would be critical to have a strong team, comprising of members having their roots in the region. In every department, brands can give preference to employees who have expertise in the language and cultural sensibilities of that specific region. Also, the managers can allow these local employees to be involved in brainstorming processes and take their inputs for content creation and strategy.

Similarly, for campaigns, brand managers can create presentations and pitch the entire campaign idea, step by step, in front of the local team members. They can validate each of the steps and understand if those content and strategy ideas would make sense to the region. There may be various monthly surveys conducted among the local team to evaluate how well the campaigns are being received by the local audience.

Also, the local team can be used to do social media listening and offer guidance on how to respond to the customer queries and serve them better, as they would know the personality traits of the regional customers better.

Similarly, monthly town hall sessions including all the members of the local team can be conducted, where contests can be conducted to come up with ideas to do better in the regional markets. And good ideas can be gratified. During the above process, valuable contributors can be shortlisted and be used significantly in decision-making processes. This way, the internal team can be motivated and used effectively to help brand growth in such regional digital markets.

(ii) External

Another method to effectively enhance the localization of content is to have stronger connections with the regional audience. Collecting regular insights and feedbacks from customers also forms a great step toward building relevant content and strategy. Some of the ways to ensure the same would include conducting various focus group discussions with regional consumers. The focus group discussions can be conducted with groups from different age groups, gender, income strata, education levels, and occupations. Such focus group discussions will help brands understand what different sects of people from the region expect from the brand. Also, they give brands a perspective of who is the target audience for their services and who is not.

It can segregate regional consumers into primary, secondary, and tertiary target groups and help to strategize their digital campaigns accordingly. The focus group discussions can be studied in detail, and among the group, persons who are contributing significantly can be identified. And as an extension, one on one interviews can be conducted in person with them.

The brand's campaigns and activities in the regional market that have been conducted so far can be reviewed on the positives and negatives. The brand's future plans can also be vetted with the interviewee, and their feedbacks could be received.

Also, the social media pages of the brand can be monitored keenly for highly engaging consumers. They can be selected as top fans of the brand in the regional market, and they can be included in a Facebook group or a WhatsApp group. The group can be administrated from the brand side, and frequent communication regarding the localizing of the services for the region can be discussed. Apart from this, local talents can be found in the form of copywriters, performers, influencers, etc., and they can be regularly involved in the content creation process.

As local talents can also give an objective perspective to brand campaigns, their inputs can act as a refreshing addition to the existing brand strategies. Always, objective third-party feedbacks are valuable under such circumstances. This process should be maintained as a continuous one. One of the main pillars a brand must use while entering a regional market is to develop friends, guides, and advocates for the brand, as they hold key in leading the light for the regional journey.

For example, one great localization campaign is from Byju's App, titled "Things Dads Say", featuring Shah Rukh Khan. It can be cited as a great example of how localization campaigns should be executed. To promote the app, which provides customized, personalized, and engaging online content to teach students, Shah Rukh Khan comes as four avatars—four dads from various regions of India (Gujarat, Punjab, Tamil Nadu, and West Bengal). In the campaign, SRK acts as a regional dad conversating with his kid based on the product, with regional cultural sensibilities on topics, issues, and bringing out the dad-child relationship; the conversations take place in various regions so that the audience from each region connects with this content and understands the product better by relating to it.

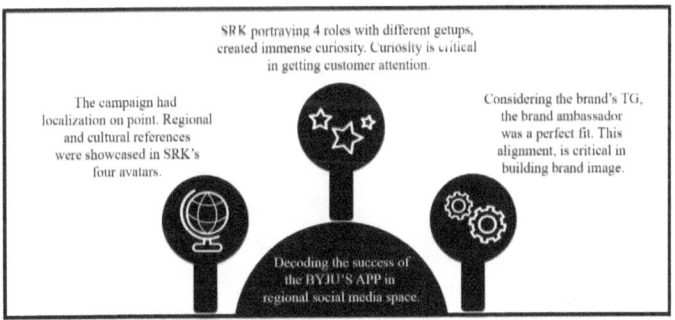

From this campaign, we can infer how localization can be effectively executed by brands to reach out to the regional audience with relatable, personalized, and customized campaigns. With this, we have come to the end of the chapter. We end with a few points for brand managers on how to create campaigns and stand-alone content pieces that are relatable to the regional audience.

Figure: Four golden rules to create relatable content.

2.5. BINGE-READ

Videos and text are two forms of content that get consumed en masse on the internet. These are very popular among the internet audience because interesting video or text content keeps users hooked to consume more and more. When users watch one video after another on the internet, it is called binge-watching. Similarly, when users read one text content after another on the internet, it is called binge-reading. The text content can be tweets, blogs, articles, reviews, infographics, customer studies, etc.

When we look at the evolution of online reading habits of users, the attention span and the time available for users to read is lesser due to the busy lifestyles. Therefore, the size of the text content has been consistently reducing, from e-papers to short articles, to blogs, to 280-character tweets, to Quora answers, and short Reddit posts.

The social media platforms have also evolved with the reading behavior of internet users. With shorter time available, and low attention span, users prefer short-form content because they can quickly skim through the gist of the content and move to other topics. If there is a topic of interest, the user chooses to read more content on the topic. With the internet, so much content is available for the user to choose at their will. Therefore, it becomes even more challenging for brands to package their content in an interesting way for users to read.

According to the Indian Readership Survey, 115 million readers across India consume news through e-papers. Around 88 percent of these users consume non-English content. Even the short text format social media platforms are very famous among Indian internet users. Twitter has around 35 million active users in India. An average Twitter user follows at least five brand accounts. In 2019, Twitter redesigned its website to help users localize content in seven Indian languages—Hindi, Gujarati, Marathi, Urdu, Tamil, Bengali, and Kannada. Twitter India said in 2019 that non-English tweets now account for half the total tweets in the country.

These data point out that regional text content has a huge potential. It shows that if a brand can put out effective text content in the form of tweets, articles, and blogs, regional users will interact, engage, and participate with the brand content. For example, during Lok Sabha Elections 2019, India saw 396 million text content being put out as tweets on election day. Such is the magnitude and potential that these social media platforms have in terms of sustaining users' interest. Regional managers should look at tapping in on such regional topics, where they can create effective text content, capitalize on the user's interest in the topic, and divert it toward the brand.

So, there is a great potential for brands to capitalize on the users' behavior of reading on the internet for long periods of time. And when it comes to regional markets, the behavior can be slightly different, as regional users prefer to read more content in their native language than English or other common languages. So, the brands focusing on regional markets can look at how to engage users with text content about the brand in regional languages. What are all the various text content formats that a brand can produce, and how can it be packaged well to attract more users? And how should it be written to keep the audience glued to the content and keep them reading one content after another?

As a brand manager entering a regional market, one should be extremely hungry for any opportunity that can be used to make effective communication about a brand and engage the audience. This is one such opportunity that can be utilized by brands entering a new regional market.

In this chapter, we will be looking at the steps a regional brand manager should take to make sure the audience binge-read their brand content. This can be done in two stages.

> 1. Packaging – First step is to make sure user gets attracted towards your content and is tempted to read your content.

> 2. Content – Second step is creating impact in your content that will make the user to continue consuming more and more content, reading – one brand content after another.

(i) Packaging

Creating text content like articles which are worth binge-reading is quite a challenge. You may have the greatest information in the article but getting a reader to read it and engage with it requires special efforts. How does the brand manager create a content strategy to create blogs or articles of their brand content and make them appeal to the user to binge-read one after another? The answer lies in how this text content is packaged and presented to users. There are various formats to package articles in an interesting manner. They are:

i. Bucket lists; for example, '7 places you should visit in Goa'. This is a format that gives the user a checklist in the form of bullet points. Since the content is given as pointers, it is easy for the user to consume, and remember. Also, such content has a great shelf life value, as many users will come back when they need quick, easy to understand information about the content.

ii. Guides; for example, '5 steps to install the software on your computer'. This is a step-by-step guide that presents content in the form of a flow chart explaining how a user should execute a function. This is also a very effective content format to transfer information quickly.

iii. Sum up; for example, '7 occasions when Sachin outsmarted the bowlers'. This is a format that is a collage of information presented in one piece. If you take the example, Sachin has a wide career, but the author is taking the effort to sum up the career under one article where the best occasions are highlighted. Similarly, a gist of large events, functions, tournaments can be highlighted in this form of content, which is easy for users to consume.

iv. Did you know format; for example, 'Do you know how to stay away from coronavirus?' This is a format that throws a question in the title and baits the user to click the article to know the answer. Typically, such articles garner a lot of reads and interest among users. However, brands should not misuse the format and end up giving clickbait articles, which will only create a bad name for the brand.

v.   Time-bound articles; for example, 'One minute read on Olympics 2021'. This is an intelligent form of content packaging. Today, users have limited time to spare. If the content is quick and easy to consume, they spend more time in reading one content after another. Taking this insight, this format is a quick read of a big news article, where a huge news item is composed into a short gist, which can be consumed in 60 seconds. If the user likes the content, they can read the next content in the series.

These are some of the content format packages that will help the user. Since the marketers are dealing with regional users, it will be better to package such content in the regional language, with regional sensibilities in terms of lingo, slang, and wordplay.

(ii) Content

Another aspect that brand managers must have a lookout for is topics that are in vogue. Sometimes certain topics suddenly generate a lot of user interest; this may be due to various reasons. Sudden happenings, situations, news, seasonal developments, etc. are some of the factors that spur a particular topic to get into vogue.

For example, the corona pandemic was a news item that led to so many topics being searched on the internet. Quarantine was suddenly a term that became famous. Content pieces that were looked at by users were food to cook in quarantine, hobbies to pursue in quarantine, books to read during quarantine, movies to watch during quarantine, etc.

Similarly, many such situations and news items will arise that will lead to a trend to be in vogue. If brand managers are aware of what people are looking out to read during a certain time period, they can produce branded content surrounding the topic to get the user's attention. This is the kind of awareness that will help brand managers keep producing regional content that regional users will find worth binge-reading.

For example, let's look at a commentary campaign run by the ESPNcricinfo website. When the Covid-19 virus shook the world, all sporting events were canceled, and cricket fans across the world were deprived of any cricket matches during this period. During the lockdown, a lot of people were inside their homes and were spending a lot of time on their mobile phones, looking at and reading up social media updates.

Cricinfo immediately sensed this opportunity and came up with a text commentary campaign on their website, which turned out to be a super hit campaign. Cricinfo chose some of the classic world cup matches which had happened in the past, when no commentary websites were present, and started doing live commentary for those matches ball by ball, giving users a virtual feel of following a classic match—as if it was happening live. Cricket fans who were bored during the lockdown found this campaign extremely interesting and started participating in it. This is a great way to produce text-based campaigns on trending regional topics.

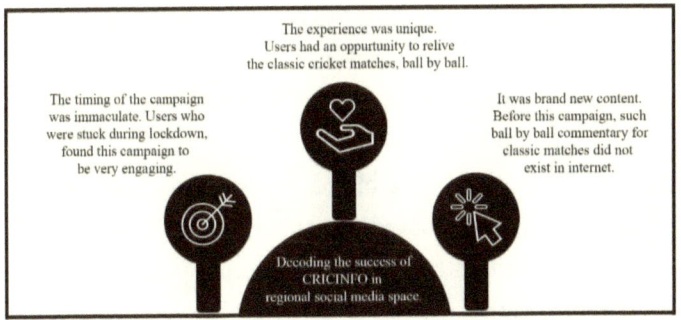

The experience was unique. Users had an oppurtunity to relive the classic cricket matches, ball by ball.

The timing of the campaign was immaculate. Users who were stuck during lockdown, found this campaign to be very engaging.

It was brand new content. Before this campaign, such ball by ball commentary for classic matches did not exist in internet.

Decoding the success of CRICINFO in regional social media space.

Similarly, whenever a brand is creating content, it is better to not create it as stand-alone content. Stand-alone contents are just one-piece articles which do not have any continuation or related articles. If a user reads a stand-alone content, there is no other content for them to follow up on, so they bounce off to another source to read content.

So, brand managers should pick a theme and create a series of content so that when a user reads one content, they should be able to read multiple articles following that; this way, a user spends more time reading articles from the brand. For example, following the success of the above campaign, Cricinfo did many more such commentary sessions with other classic matches, to make the campaign into a series. Also, inspired by the Cricinfo campaign, many sports brands like some IPL teams tried to do commentary-based cricket match campaigns on Twitter.

There are various content formats for brand managers to create a series of content.

(i) Episodic content – It follows a sequential format of one article leading to another.

(ii) Follow-up content – It gives an update or latest addition to an article that was posted before. If the user had read the previous article, they would be interested in reading a follow-up.

(iii) Original series – If a brand creates a series of its own, like a celebrity-based series or format-based series, where the content follows a similar prototype, users keep consuming one text content after another, as they follow a similar pattern. For example, interview format, Q&A with a celebrity, etc.

(iv) Author series – If a brand has various authors working on its branded content, articles written by the same author can be clubbed into one series. The writing style of the author will get the user's interest to keep reading.

(v) Topic-based – Clubbing together various branded content based on the same topics as a series. Users who read branded content about a particular topic of their interest will be interested to read more stories about the same topic.

These are some of the ways to keep getting the user to binge-read the brand's content. One effective way of getting regional users to visit your brand website is to keep writing blogs and articles on the website about regional topics so that the SEO of the website gets improved and the website's rank keeps improving as more and more regional users open the website to read the content. The more blogs are updated about the latest topics, the more active the website is. The more active the website is, the more chances for it to show up on search engine sites. It will be good for brand managers to have their sites come up in the top position when a regional user searches for related content.

So, we have come to the end of the chapter. The takeaway from this chapter is a chart highlighting the steps to create text content that is binge-worthy.

Figure: How to create binge-worthy text content.

2.6. SURFING PATTERNS

A brand manager must be omniscient of their user's behavior on the internet. They should be thoroughly aware of –

(i) Who their followers are,

(ii) Where they come from,

(iii) What they like,

(iv) What they dislike,

(v) Why do they follow our brand,

(vi) What do they expect of our brand,

(vii) What kind of relationship do they have with the brand,

(viii) What else apart from the brand do they like,

(ix) How loyal are they toward the brand,

(x) How engaged are they with the brand,

(xi) For how long have they been followers of the brand,

(xii) What are their experiences with the brand so far.

Consider your brand's online presence to be a sea full of brand content. We can make the surfing experience better only when you know who is surfing in it, where he is surfing, what time he is surfing, how long he is surfing, and why he is surfing. In short, only when a brand manager knows their brand's followers, they can provide them appropriate information.

If a brand manager is well aware of their followers and their behaviors, it becomes easier to plot the customer lifecycle and how to yield better results from the customer toward the brand in terms of engagement and purchases.

Converting a passive customer to an active customer. Active customer to a loyal customer. When brand managers are aware of such a break up of details about their followers, it can be easier to plan specific campaigns for each audience set to achieve specific targets.

Similarly, when the managers know in which parts of the region their brand is strong and in which parts the following is weak, appropriate efforts can be directed to concentrate on the various strengths and weaknesses of the brand in terms of regional following. And suitably, the various opportunities and threats can be handled for the brand in regional markets.

In this chapter, we will be looking at the steps a regional brand manager should take to know who their followers are and how to engage them better to achieve brand objectives. This can be done in three stages.

1. Audit – Audit about the followers, their demographics, behaviors, purchase intentions, motivation factors and current relationship with brand.

2. SW – Audit on strengths, weakness of the brand in regional market depending on the current following and brand presence.

3. OT - Analyzing of various opportunities that brand can tap based on the strengths and the various threats, the brand needs to tackle based on the weakness.

(i) Audit

Auditing your social media presence is a critical process in digital media marketing. Only by knowing the present situation of the brand's digital media presence, the manager can plan on setting targets and growing it to the next stage. When a brand enters a regional market, some of the major decisions brand managers would need to take are regarding whether the brand needs separate regional pages or can one main page of the brand cater to all regional markets.

(a) If only one page is going to cater to all the markets.
(b) How can specific posts for specific regions be targeted?
(c) Is it advantageous to have one cumulative repository of all the brand's followers? Or
(d) Keeping the pages separate from each other and having different strategies for each will serve the brand better?

To answer these questions, the brand manager should first audit the current followers of the page, where they are from, how many of them are regional language users, how many of them are mobile users, and how many of them engage with the page regularly. These details can be found through various analytical tools. To start with, each platform such as Facebook, Twitter, etc. has inbuilt analytical tools for pages to show basic details about the page. But there are limited tools to explore competitor pages in these analytics.

There are analytical tools such as CrowdTangle to measure competitor performance, market performance, and the best performing posts. With these tools, many insights can be attained. Managers can earmark industry average numbers for the number of followers, engagements, video views, and brand name mentions.

This would be useful to plan campaigns and budgets for building the page. The traffic coming to your brand's website can be analyzed using tools such as Google Analytics, through which important data like the source of the traffic, the average time spent per visit, from which part of the region most visits are coming, bounce rate of various pages inside the website, average watch time of videos, number of pages navigated by the user can all be analyzed.

However, a research study by DBD Media states that 30 percent of companies do not have a dedicated team or person set up to do web analysis for their brands. 67 percent of companies do not track their social media networks, making it difficult to track where their content is being shared and by whom. 73 percent of companies do not measure their online goals and actions accurately, leaving it difficult to understand who their customers are, from where they came, and what was their purchase intention or behavior pattern.

All these data are important for a brand manager to deeply investigate the consumer behavior of the regional user and understand him in-depth so that the communication about the brand's products and services can be delivered to them in an appropriate style.

(ii) SWOT

Once the audit is completed and a process is set up to measure the key metrics of the regional digital media presence of the brand, various strengths and weaknesses of the brand in the digital space can be explored by the manager. For instance, the strengths of the brand can be identified by two factors: stars and cash cow.

a. The star element of a brand's digital media presence can be seen as the one greatest power the brand possesses that keeps propelling and positively gratifying the brand in the regional digital space. The star factor can be the brand's content, the brand's ambassador, the brand's mascots, the influencers, events, or even some of the fans who actively advocate and share the brand's posts with their network and help the brand grow. So, the brand manager should identify which aspect of the digital presence is working really well for the brand and try to maintain the momentum. For example, short-form video content like live videos and boomerang videos from the brand's mascot which get great engagement for star value.

b. Similarly, there is something called as a cash cow, which is not as powerful as the star element. But it keeps bringing constant and consistent incremental growth to the brand every day. Star elements are flashy and may be expensive for the brands. But cash cows are the organic, day-to-day activities that keep the brand growing steadily. Brand managers should explore and identify cash cows to keep the brand's growth consistent. With the elements of strength, the brand can identify the various opportunities it has to grow further. Managers can plan various campaigns to use the elements of strength better and seize various opportunities. For example, long-form video content like daily astrology which keeps giving constant views every day but does not perform extraordinarily.

Similarly, the weaknesses of the digital presence of the brands can also be identified by two factors. Some aspects of the brand's content strategy would require too much budget and too much effort from the manager and team. These aspects would have been thought of by the brand managers as stars. However, these aspects may not produce the results that were expected of them. These elements would have had high potential, but for some reason, because of some internal and external issues, they would not have succeeded. These elements are called the question marks.

For example, this may be the brand's call to action content like a lucky draw for special discounts. The content may be good, but it may not get the desired action from customers. If this content works, the engagement levels can be boosted for the brand. Then, the brand manager and team should explore which part of the strategy is the bottleneck and try to rectify it.

And there would be some elements in the process that do not have potential and are not giving any returns also. They should be identified and discontinued by the managers, as those efforts can be invested somewhere else. For example, these content formats may not have connection, relevance, or relativity with the regional user and are getting ignored by them. By identifying these weaknesses and appropriately acting on the insights, brand managers can prevent brands from facing any upcoming threats.

So, we have come to the end of the chapter. The takeaway from this chapter is a chart highlighting the successful ways to conduct an audit and plot the strengths and weaknesses of the brand.

Figure: How to do a SWOT analysis for your digital media strategy.

WINNING THE REGIONAL DIGITAL CONSUMER - PART 2

With the first six chapters on how to win the regional consumer, we focused on the information transfer. We discussed various strategies and techniques of understanding the regional user's need to attain new information, updates about various topics, and sharing it with their friends. We discussed the ways regional managers can create a content calendar on how to satisfy the user's need to get gratified by the attainment of new information by providing them information through many content formats.

We had discussed that as a digital marketer, there are two routes to a customer's heart. So, in this section of the book, we will be looking at winning the regional customer through entertainment gratification. We will be looking at studying the taste, likes, dislikes of the regional user and then creating various content strategies and techniques to keep them entertained with the brand content. We will be discussing how to come up with various content ideas to entertain users with fun content and provide a temporary break from their everyday stress and problems in reality.

Some of the questions answered in this chapter are as follows:

1. How do we identify the regional user's leisure interests?
2. How do we get the user to choose our page over others for his entertainment need?
3. How do we get the user to talk about our content in his social groups (WOM)?
4. How do we get the user to influence his network also to try out our content?
5. How do we get the user to spend more time with our content?
6. How do we get the user to engage and contribute by giving inputs to our content?
7. How to identify other popular content creators who provide entertainment in this region?
8. How to get the user to be involved and generate content based on the brand's needs and requirements?
9. How to recommend relatable and suitable content to a regional user according to the latest regional trends?
10. What is going to be my regional content strategy, and how to compose the content calendar?

It is critical for digital marketers to craft an effective content strategy with content formats that will help brands engage with users actively, entertain them, and further share it to reach a new audience to establish growth in the market. In this section, there are six chapters to guide brand managers and digital marketers on how to achieve the desired objectives regarding information transfer.

3.1. ATTENTION ECONOMY

One major thing that digital marketers need to understand is that in digital media, the most valuable currency is a user's attention. That's because, in their busy lives, users have limited time to spare for leisure activities, and internet consumption is a part of it. During internet consumption also, the amount of attention the user gives to content differs from one case to another.

We can classify internet consumption into active internet consumption, where a user actively engages with content and participates. For example, intense reading of an internet article and learning new information. And passive consumption, where the content gets played in the background and the user gets involved in some other activity. For example, playing songs on YouTube in the background and working. The intensity of attention in the two cases differs. Similarly, due to many distractions and the availability of too much content on the internet, the user's attention span and the intensity of the attention they give to content are very unpredictable. That makes it the most important and critical resource for brands on the internet.

Let us look at some data points to put things into context. According to InMobi's 2020 Mobile Marketing Handbook for India, Indian internet users have the highest per capita internet consumption in the world (9.8 GB/User/Month). Smartphones have accelerated internet penetration and consumption in India. By 2022, 64 percent of Indians will be connected to the internet through smartphones. 87 percent of rural consumers are online through mobile phones. India is showing 5x growth in content consumption on the internet.

These are all great numbers, but because there has been such an internet explosion and content accessibility, users are becoming impatient and impulsive. Their attention span toward a content drastically reduced to a mere 8 seconds in 2018. Therefore, within 8 seconds, brand managers and content creators have to convey powerful content to make the user stay. This is because of the immense amount of content options before users and their multi-tasking lifestyle.

This job is tougher for regional brand managers, as attracting a regional user within 8 seconds in a new market is going to be difficult. 72 percent of marketers feel that their biggest challenge in the coming days is going to be understanding the regional markets and user preference. 45 percent feel building vernacular/regional/customized experiences will be a challenge.

Since the attention of a user on the internet is a scarce resource, every brand in the digital media space fights for a piece of the cake. When a brand enters the regional market, this becomes an even tougher challenge for the manager, as in the new terrain, it would be far more difficult to compete for attention with local brands and other competitors who have spent more time in the regional markets before.

In this chapter, we will be looking at the steps a regional brand manager should take to capture their share of users' attention in the social media space and how they can effectively measure and manage their share of attention. This can be done in two stages.

> **1. Presence** – First step is being available, being present in the platforms for the user to discover the brand

> **2. Impact** – Second step is creating impact in your content to make users actively engage with your content and increase the brand's share of user attention.

(i) Presence

The first step in grabbing your share of users' attention in digital media is making sure that you are present in the right places. Only when a brand is accessible and discoverable for a user, it would get the much-needed attention from them. So, how does a brand manager make sure that their brand is present in the right places to get the user's attention? There is a three-pronged strategy that they can follow: content, consistency, and positioning.

(i) **Content** – The first part of making a great presence in digital marketing deals with how well the content is created and presented. For this, the brand manager must be well aware of the topic, genre, format, style, etc. that is in the trend in the regional market. Based upon the same, the content calendar can be created and suitable content for each platform can be created for the brand. For example, if the summer season is about to start in the region, various topical, engaging content related to the summer season can be created for the brand. So, when a user searches anything related to summer, the brand's content is present for him to consume.

The brand manager must do regular checks on the current trending topics and create attention arresting content for the brands to keep growing their share of users' attention in the regional digital space.

(ii) **Consistency** – The second important step is being consistent. Brands cannot afford to have a flash in the pan kind of approach, as it would be very difficult to retain a significant presence in the digital space with inconsistency. It is critical for the brand to follow a content strategy that has a pattern. For example, a content posting pattern can be like two content pieces a day, one in the morning and one in the evening. This kind of strategy maximizes the brand content's visibility to users.

For example, Madan Gowri, a YouTuber from Tamil Nadu, consistently posts one video per day in the evenings. He picks a topic relevant to the audience on a particular day, does some basic research, and explains his understandings to his audience every day. In a matter of a couple of years, the channel grew to 3.5 million subscribers. The biggest reason for his success is the consistency of his videos, his consistent video making style, and the consistent release timing. The audience got tuned to this habit and waited for his video to drop every evening to learn about a new topic.

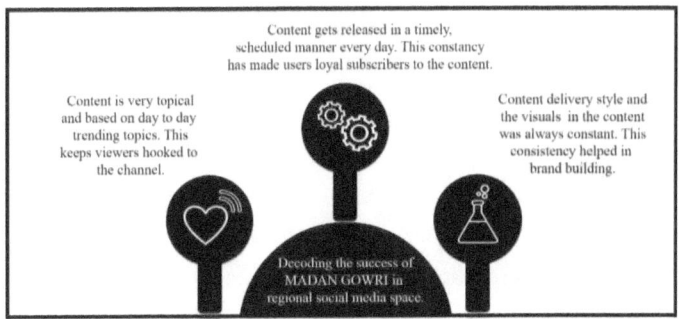

(iii) **Positioning** – The third step is positioning. As much as content and consistency, how you position the content on the social media platform is very important. Content gets discovered by search, display, and suggestions. Brand managers should implement effective SEO (search engine optimization) and SEM (search engine marketing) tactics to get their content easily discovered and ranked up when a user searches for any topic that is related to the brand content. By using tools and best keywords related to the region, the topic and content can be searched and used.

Similarly, brands can place ads on Google to place their content while the user searches for a popular topic. Title and thumbnail should be designed in a manner that attracts clicks and attention. Similarly, each content should not be projected as stand-alone content; instead, it should be projected as a series, where one content leads to another. And the similar important keywords of this content should be added in the other so that the next to next content of the brand is shown as suggestions. These are some of the ways that brand managers can effectively create a presence for their brand content.

(ii) Impact

The next step in securing and maximizing the attention time span of the user is to create a solid impact with the content. The content created by the brand should be able to hold the user's attention to the maximum time span possible before letting them go to consume other content. Metrics such as video watch time and website bounce rate are important because of this factor. The more watch time a user consumes, the more the share of attention that is garnered by the brand. The more the attention given by the user, the more likely he is to engage and stay loyal to the brand. The factors of content that create more impact on users are relatability and stickiness.

The more relatable the content is to the user, the more they get connected to it. For example, if it is video content, the characters in the video should be able to touch a chord with the user so that the user is able to feel the emotions of the character and is interested to know what will happen to the character, as the content keeps running from one video to another.

Similarly, if it's text content, the user should be able to relate and drown in the writing of the content so much so that they cannot break away from the content in the middle. The second part of creating an impact is to produce content that has a great stickiness value to it. What do we mean by stickiness? The ability of the content to hold the user for the longest time possible. How to create stickiness? By pacing the content evenly from start to end so that the interest level does not drop through the content. Sometimes brands, in order to get the user to consume content quickly, reveal all the important details of the content in the first few seconds of consumption. The user, who has already consumed the gist of the content, bounces off to another content. That's why it is necessary to pace the content evenly from the start, middle, and end. Once we break the content into three parts and spread out the interesting details evenly, the user stays longer.

With a great hook-line, the content can grab the attention of the user. The middle part of the content should keep building up to the climax. The end part of the content should end on a high, with a twist that leads to another content. This way, the user gives more attention to the content. And brand managers can secure the maximum share of user attention through this strategy.

So, we have come to the end of the chapter. The takeaway from this chapter is a few points on how to create content that can hold the user's attention for a longer time.

Figure: How to create content that can hold attention for a longer time period.

3.2. PARASOCIAL RELATIONSHIPS

In a country like ours, celebrities such as actors and public personalities are considered to be larger than life and are celebrated widely. For instance, the impact that actors create when they appear on large screens makes people relate to their performances so much. The audience relates to them so much that they tend to cheer for them when they bash villains, mouth punch dialogues, and cry when there is an emotional scene. This is the power of the visual medium.

The bond between a celebrity and the audience extends from the virtual life to even real life. Have you come across crowds flocking the streets to catch a glimpse of a celebrity, trying to get autographs, photographs, and even sharing photos clicked on their phones to their social network, saying that they saw a celebrity that day? This is called parasocial relationships.

It is a one-sided relationship that the audience shares with celebrities, relating to them on a personal level even though they have never met or spent time with them in real life. This kind of parasocial relationship even exists in the digital world. Have you ever come across Twitter or Instagram accounts of celebrities, the number of likes they receive for each post? The huge amount of personal affection and love they receive in the comment section. The number of people who throng to get a peek of their personal lives and ask them questions when they go live from their social media pages. This kind of consumer behavior is even higher in regional markets, as the internet is the only access for them to reach out to their larger-than-life celebrities.

This relationship is also very evident in digital media. People develop bonds with celebrities and personalities that they see in internet videos. The impact of their relationship is made use of by brands to achieve their desired objectives by using celebrity-led influencer campaigns and brand endorsements. In India, these celebrity campaigns find more relevance, given the mass fan following commanded by Indian celebrities.

Duff & Phelps, in their report, state that close to 50 percent of endorsements in India feature celebrities, as compared to around 20 percent in the U.S. Over the past decade, the number of celebrity-led endorsements have increased from 650 ads in 2007 to 1660 ad campaigns in 2017, representing a steady compounded annual growth rate (CAGR) of 10 percent. Indian celebrities have also adopted digital media well, and command followers to the tune of few millions across platforms, which can be capitalized by the brands for their campaigns.

In this chapter, we will be looking at various methods through which brand managers can capitalize on this user behavior. How should a brand effectively run campaigns featuring celebrities? How should a brand manager choose which celebrity they should work with in the regional campaigns? And how should the campaigns be structured to effectively leverage the parasocial bond that a celebrity has with the audience? There are two steps a manager has to ensure to ace the celebrity campaigns for regional markets.

1. Connect – How to make the perfect connect between the brand, the celebrity and the content for the campaign to click with the audience.

2. Action – How to measure and ensure the effort spent on the campaign yields the right results for the brand in the regional market?

(i) Connect

Have you ever come across advertisements where celebrities endorse products that are completely unrelated to them? Have you ever come across advertisements where celebrities appear in content that is completely not their style, the way they usually communicate or act in movies? These are the result of the mismatches that happen when a brand manager chooses the wrong celebrity to endorse their brand.

Most often than not, brand managers are strangled by various limitations in terms of budgets, in terms of celebrity availability, in terms of timing issues, etc. to choose celebrities to endorse their products in advertisements. This kind of campaign solves no purpose; neither does it bring goodwill to the brand nor does it bring any connection with the audience, which it was intended to.

The same applies to digital media. When employing celebrities and influencers to shout-out for the brands on their social media pages, the brand managers must ensure that there is a synergy between the chosen celebrity with the brand as well as the content they are putting out. Some points that managers need to note are: What is the celebrity famous for? Are there any style quotients, personality quotients, content-related assets such as punch dialogues and regional catchphrases that the celebrity is known for? Is there a pattern with which the celebrity posts their social media content? What is the tone of the language used by the celebrity in their posts? How connected is the celebrity with the audience? What is the level of the bond that the celebrity shares with their fans? What is the level of influence that the celebrity has on their audience's purchasing decisions? Has the celebrity endorsed any other brands or products on their social media profiles before? Are those brands/products similar to our brand or competitors to our brand? Brand managers must keep a list of such questions and explore various options of celebrities who would be the right candidate to be the voice of the brand in the regional campaigns.

For example, filmmaker Karan Johar sported a gray hair look during the COVID-19 lockdown. He was constantly joking about his aging, and the gray hair look of his demanded father roles. Godrej hair dye made use of this opportunity and came up with a great campaign to give Karan Johar a new look on his birthday. The brand used Karan Johar's situation as an opportunity to showcase the product's functionality. Karan Johar tried out the dye for the first time; his new dashing look and his reactions for the same were captured in a beautiful selfie candid video. This was a great influencer campaign, as it did not look forced and served the brand's purpose.

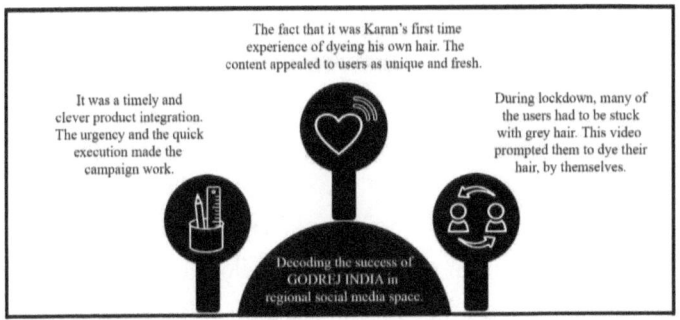

Depending on the choice of the celebrity, the content for the campaign should be carefully crafted so that the campaign does not look like a force fit. The content should be in synergy with the voice and characteristics of the celebrity so that it organically fits in and makes a connection with their audience. Elements such as symbolism, references, catchphrases, song lyrics, etc. from the celebrity's previous creations can be woven in the content so that the campaign effectively makes use of the parasocial relationship the celebrity has with their fans; these elements have played a significant role in building that relationship in the first place.

These are some of the things that brand managers must consider while creating campaigns and content that effectively leverage the celebrity's clout in the regional digital space.

(ii) Action

A parasocial relationship is a one-way relationship between a fan and a celebrity. It is not quantifiable. The bond that a fan shares with the celebrity and the influence the celebrity has on the various customer decisions vary from one case to another.

Firstly, the clout that a celebrity has is again not a quantified one and is subjective. It is left to the manager's perspective to measure how much of a hold a celebrity has on his audience. For instance, we can say how many followers a celebrity has or how many likes they receive for a post. But we can never say with the same conviction and authority how many of their fans will go buy a product if the celebrity endorses one.

We can argue that past campaigns can be taken as a measure and historical evidence can be used as a yardstick to measure a celebrity's influence over the purchase decision of their fans. However, that is a tricky proposition, given the amount of money and effort needed to pull out a successful celebrity integration for a brand campaign. The risks are even higher for a digital media campaign, as further complications such as the celebrity's digital media presence, their page strength, engagement metrics also come into the picture while measuring how effective a celebrity shout-out will be for delivering the brand's objectives.

It is also imperative to see whether the parasocial bond shared with a fan is effectively extended to digital media by the celebrity. So, under these circumstances, how does a brand manager make sure that the effort spent on the campaign yields the right results for the brand in the regional market? The answer lies in the question.

A parasocial relationship is non-quantifiable in nature; however, when the brand manager plans for a celebrity-driven regional campaign, there must be an effective call to action that should be the central piece of it. Say, a website to register, a phone number to call, a Google document to fill, a YouTube channel to subscribe to, a link to purchase the product, or a referral discount code to use while purchasing—there should be an effective landing page, the end result of the campaign that should be measurable. When an end deliverable has been effectively devised, it becomes relatively easy for the manager to divert all the effort of this campaign toward it.

For example, there are many challenges that were given by celebrities to their followers such as bottle cap open challenge (open a bottle's cap by kicking it), mannequin challenge (freeze and take a video), 10-year photo challenge (upload two pictures; a current one and one from 10 years ago). These are all great call to action campaigns in which people will actively participate. Brand managers should work out such interesting call to action campaigns that will get regional users to jump in and participate!

So, the process becomes more tenable now. Starting from writing the content for the campaign, involving punch lines and catchphrases of the celebrity, to boosting the campaign with ad spends—the entire process can be structured to direct the audience toward the end deliverable. This way, the results can be measured, and the manager can measure how well the efforts have yielded results for the brand and make rational decisions on carrying forward with regional campaigns that involve celebrity integrations.

So, we have come to the end of the chapter. The takeaway from this chapter is a checklist of how one can use celebrities effectively in their brand campaigns.

Figure: How to utilize celebrities effectively in a brand campaign.

3.3. BINGE-WATCHING

Since the advent of high internet penetration and cheap internet costs, there has been a phenomenal increase in online video consumption among internet users. More than two billion videos are streamed on YouTube daily. And nearly 75 percent of internet traffic is occupied by video streaming. In India, recently, Hotstar in its report has said 40 percent of its video consumption is of regional content. And around 63 percent of the consumption comes from tier 2, tier 3 cities.

The major reason for this kind of phenomenon is the user's intention and liking toward binge-watching behavior. A video is an effective form of content format that has high retentive value with a user. The user spends more time watching video content than any other content format.

Binge-watching is nothing but watching internet videos one after another. How many times have you gone to YouTube to just watch one song video but end up spending hours together on YouTube, watching multiple videos one after another? This kind of behavior is very common in regional markets, as the internet is one of the most accessible and affordable forms of entertainment for them.

In this chapter, we will be looking at two strategies to use and capitalize on this binge-watching behavior of the regional users. Using these two strategies, we will look to maximize the brand's share in the user's mind space.

A. Push Strategy - Pushing the Video content towards audience to binge watch.

B. Pull Strategy – Pulling the users towards binge watching the brand content.

(i) Push Strategy

When a brand enters a regional market, they will have to start building their digital media presence from scratch. During the initial stages, the brand will tend to have limited reach among followers due to low exposure and awareness in the market. Especially during this stage, the brand managers must employ various push strategies to push the brand's video content toward the users. Push strategy enables brand managers to take the video content and drop it to the user to ensure exposure. This kind of strategy helps brand managers to have complete control of the ecosystem, ensuring the reach of the video to the targeted audience.

One main method of this strategy is push notifications. Push notifications are alert messages that are given to the user's mobile phones as a form of text message or notification. The user gets a message that the brand has released a new video and to click to watch it. This kind of notification ensures that users are given an alert message about the video so that they do not miss it. Some effective ways of making use of this feature are using nice regional catchwords and punch dialogues as alert messages so that the user clicks the notification and watches the video. Once the user watches the video content, they can be expected to watch one video after another from the brand page.

Another method is to execute retargeting advertisements. The brand manager must analyze their video content and compare for similar, competing, related videos in the market. And when such videos are identified, they must effectively place advertisements of their videos for the users who had previously consumed their competitor's content.

This is a very effective method of advertising, as we know that the user likes and prefers to watch similar content. Therefore, he is more likely to click and consume the video content that is presented as an advertisement. Similarly, ads on YouTube or other video streaming platforms can be targeted to place the brand's video right next to popular videos that are in the same segment.

For example, our brand video is a video about taking care of a newborn baby. This brand video can be placed right next to popular baby videos on the internet of the regional space. This can be done through effective targeting and retargeting advertisement tactics. The whole idea behind this is getting the user to consume one video and depend on his binge-watching behavior to watch one video after another from the brand page thereafter.

(ii) Pull Strategy

In this part of the chapter, we will be looking at the various strategies that a brand manager can use to pull the audience toward the video content. It is common logic that when a user willingly makes an effort to consume content, they spend more time watching it, and the retentive rates are very high, as well as the bounce rates are comparatively lower. This is because the decision to watch the content has been driven by a user motive. Therefore, it is wise for brand managers to also have effective pull strategies to motivate a user to come and click their content, rather than only pushing the links for them to consume. So, how can the user be motivated to binge-watch a brand's content?

One must take a lot of care in how you display your video to the audience. How you package the video, how the video is presented, at what time is it presented, how long is the content, does the video look aesthetically well made, is the video cut well enough to hold the audience's interest, is the video focusing on regional sensibilities? These are qualitative questions that the brand managers must ensure with content creators and distributors. They should do a thorough check on the making of the video and how the video is positioned, promoted, and released.

Positioning is about answering the question - What purpose is the video serving? It can involve factors such as the video can be a stand-alone video or a part of a campaign, can be made on a trending topic, can be made based out of a user requirement. Promotion factors can include creating organic posts, updates about teasers of the video, releasing countdown posters, releasing first look posters, releasing photos, screenshots from the video, releasing few content bytes from artists, characters involved in the video.

Such tactics will build the expectation of the video. Therefore, it will increase awareness about the video as well as consumption of content related to the video. Also, brand managers should look at their page characteristics on when there is a lot of traction in the page, at what time their users interact, what are the dynamics of the audience in terms of gender, profession, and usage behavior, and accordingly the release strategy of the video should be decided. One more strategy that can pull the audience toward content is using hashtags and keywords.

Brand managers must realize that the internet is like space; there are various clusters of content present all over the space. Users are like travelers who keep moving around the space to consume content. It is up to the managers to make sure that their video content is placed in the pathway of the intended travelers. For this purpose, hashtags and keywords are used.

Hashtags and keywords are like maps for the websites to understand where the brand's content belongs in the space. For example, a famous hashtag is #MondayMotivations. It deals with motivational content for users to watch before starting a week. In the same way, #FridayFeelings or #TGIF (Thank God, it's Friday) are hashtags used to celebrate the arrival of the much-needed weekend after a tiring week. One more hashtag that is very famous among internet users is #OOTD (Outfit of the day), where users upload their look or wardrobe that they are sporting to work or a function or an event.

Similarly, brand managers must inspect what are the hashtags and keywords that are famous in the region they are venturing into and try to create content revolving the same. For instance, #Kolaveri (murderous rage) became a super trending topic in Tamil Nadu after a Tamil song became a viral hit. People used that hashtag to vent out their anger on various things on social media. Such regional insights can help brand managers immensely. Twitter states that brands can increase their engagements by 50 percent by using appropriate hashtags that are relevant to their content.

When the managers enter the regional keywords which are related to the video, the content gets placed among similar regional content appropriately. Managers can look at similar videos as well as competitor videos and use various keyword tools to make note of which keywords are popular in the region, language, and culture which are related to the video. After doing that, they can make use of such keywords for the video. This way, the video gets placed appropriately in the regional social media space.

Why are tags important? There are thousands and thousands of contents uploaded on a social media platform like YouTube every day. For the platform, your content is just another piece of video. Only when we feed in the appropriate title, tags, description, keywords about the content, inside the platform, the platform understands what this content is about, to which users this content will be appropriate, and next to which existing videos it can be placed.

For example, your video is about how to bake a cake using your company's product. When keywords such as cake, baking, chocolate cake, cake baking ideas, etc. are inserted in the content, the brand's video can be shown to users who are searching for content related to baking. Simply put, your tags and keywords help the platform find you the right audience for your content.

Similarly, while working on regional content, brand managers can find out regional keywords and tags that are relevant, popular, and appropriate for your content. Once the content lands in the regional customer's pathway, the binge-watching behavior of the customer can be relied on to watch more videos from the brand page and then become a loyal digital viewer.

So, we have come to the end of this chapter. The takeaway from the chapter is a chart that showcases some of the best practices to keep your regional customers glued to your content and binge-watch your brand videos. You can use them as a checklist to verify if you are catering to these points in your content strategy!

Figure: Four golden rules to get users attracted to your content.

3.4. COMPANIONSHIP

Many research studies show that users who spend long hours on the internet do it to deal with loneliness. Loners and introverts compensate for their limited social interactions with spending a longer time on the internet by binge-watching and binge-surfing. Also, communicating via social networking platforms such as Facebook and WhatsApp is far more convenient and easier for lonely people.

According to a study conducted by the Pew Research Center, 54 percent of users said they text their friends at least once a day, while only 33 percent said they talk face-to-face with their friends on a consistent basis. The inhibitions and barriers they face during face-to-face communications disappear when they are behind a laptop or a mobile phone. Therefore, talking out their mind by spending more time in conversations becomes easier. This phenomenon also works well in building bonds with onscreen characters and identifying with them. Relating to certain online characters as themselves and connecting with them is also a common practice among loners.

How many of you watch the TV series 'Friends' and relate to the characters Rachel, Ross, Joey, Chandler, and Monica? The absence of friends in real life is compensated by befriending online characters, and spending time with them by binge-watching shows is a common behavior among internet users. The users become so involved with the characters that they stay attached to the series to know what happens next. Morning Consult, in its study, suggests that 76 percent of internet users admit to staying all night to watch a tv show. 45 percent accept that they have even canceled social plans like dinner with family and friends to spend more time watching video series.

These statistics show that the impact the internet creates on providing companionship to users is very huge. The internet is a very addictive medium; it has evolved from a place that provides only entertainment to a place where it gives company and personal bonding to users. Such behavior is a common phenomenon and is also prevalent among regional internet users. If the millennial urban audience is attached to Joey and Ross of 'Friends', the regional audience has the same attachment toward their serial actors and 'Bigg Boss' participants.

Do you remember the rage 'Bigg Boss' participant Oviya generated among the Tamil audience? So many Tamil fans started the Oviya army, voting in support of her during elimination, bashing and trolling her opponents, staying online to catch a glimpse of the promos and episodes as soon as it was released, and tweeting in support of her. That is the potential of the companionship internet and online content can have on a user. Thus, it can be seen that the need for companionship exists at a high magnitude among regional internet users.

In this chapter, we will be looking at the steps a regional brand manager should take to make the brand and its content become a companion to regional users. By understanding the emotional needs of the regional user, brand managers can devise content plans and strategies to provide companionship to regional users and thereby build an inseparable bond with the regional users. Companionship can be built in the digital world in almost the same way of getting to know someone in real life.

> 1. Icebreaker – Breaking the barriers between user and the brand by coming out with shattering 'first conversation' campaign. The brand by these campaigns extend their hands to get to know the user.

> 2. Conversations Builder – Engaging with users regularly with fun and engaging content that will result in spending quality time with the brand posts. Call to action posts, contests, etc. are some of the methods to keep the conversations warm.

(i) Ice Breaker

The first step of getting to develop a bond with the regional audience is to break the ice. When a brand enters a new regional market that it has never ventured into before, the users in the regional market would not exactly know who the brand is, what they are about, and how they will communicate on their digital platforms. There will be a sense of void-ness in the air during the initial phase of the launch. The brand manager should try to break the ice between the brand and the user as quickly and effectively as they can to keep the brand's digital communications fluid. Only when a user feels comfortable, they would start engaging and conversating with brands on digital media.

Only when this communication is enabled, the brand can start listening to suggestions, feedbacks, and reviews from regional users on how to improve the products and services for the regional market. So, how can the ice be broken? The first step is to introduce the brand effectively to the user. This is us; this is what we do, this is what we have done in other markets, this is what we plan to do here. This kind of a good introduction in the form of logo reveal videos, company profile videos, brand reveal videos, anthems, or advertisements can be a good start so that the audience will get to know who they are getting connected to.

For example, Colors TV, when it launched its Colors Tamil tv channel, came up with a brand song called 'Namma Ooru Coloru', relating to how Tamil Nadu's colors are going to be reflected in its tv shows. Since Colors TV is a national brand, regionalization was done through this beautiful video showcasing Tamil Nadu's iconic elements such as Jallikattu, temples, Marina Beach, kolams, Bharatanatyam, etc. This was a great introduction video about the brand to its new market and audience.

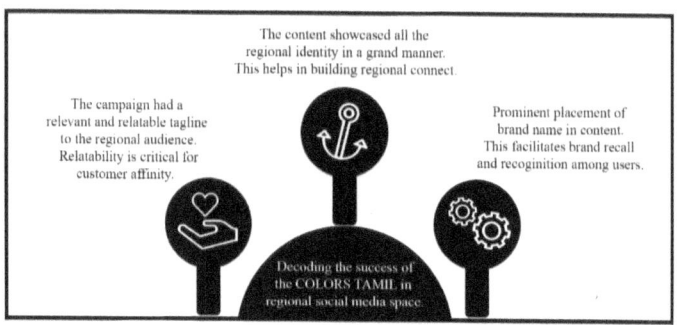

The next step is to humanize the brand's presence so that the user feels comfortable to open up and connect with the brand's communications. The brand manager should look at creating a positive environment by encouraging the user to interact with the brand—like their comments, respond to their posts with a personalized comment instead of an automated reply, greet them, and make them feel welcomed to the page.

Some campaigns that can induce positivity and encourage user involvement would be asking users to send selfies of them using the products of the brand. And each selfie can be gratified with free brand merchandise, gift vouchers, or celebrity autographed gifts. This way, users will be encouraged to check out the product and interact with the brand by sending their reviews and selfies. Such activities can induce the user to make the first interactions with the brand. Also, the brand can follow up on conversations with the user on their reviews and feedbacks, keep them updated that the brand really cares about their opinions. With this, the ice between the brand and the regional user is truly melted and is now warm for more conversations.

(ii) Conversation Builder

Once the ice between the brand and the user is broken, the next step is to build meaningful conversations to make the bond stronger. This needs to be done to keep the relationship warm and active. The more the conversations and engagement happen between the user and the brand, the stronger the bond. How does a manager ensure this? The answer lies in coming up with an effective content strategy that is consistent and continuous.

The brand managers must come out with a manual on how to deal with customer conversations. Should there be a format or a style in which the replies should be made? Or should it be organic and natural? Should the communication style of the brand remain consistent in all conversations, or should it be fluid and on the go? These are brand guidelines that need to be penned before brands start building conversations with the user. Also, the important thing that the brand must keep in mind while conversating with the user is how much is too much? How much content should the brand reveal, how personal should the brand get with the user, what are the lines that the brand should not cross, and when should the brand place a full stop?

Conversations with consumers are like gold dust—it is amazing to sprinkle it when necessary, but when overused, it looks ugly. Similarly, the brand manager should devise certain guidelines on how the brand should react during a crisis communication; for example, dealing with an angry customer, a troll, or negative comments on the post.

Crisis communication is an art. More often than not, the customer we are conversating with would be in a negative mind state—angry, distressed, and unhappy. At that time, automated messaging or messaging without an action or purpose would further irritate the customer. Therefore, the response should be quick, but the response should also be backed by action. For example, rectifying the order or refunding the money if the customer faced a bad product experience.

Similarly, the language, tonality, and the response timing of the messages must be filled with empathy and care so that the customer feels safe. More often than not, all that the angry customer needs the brand to be is a good listener who can listen to their queries and their experiences. After listening and quickly escalating the issues to the respective business units, the digital team should follow up and make sure remedial solutions are delivered to the customer. The circle gets fulfilled only when the customer who complained on the brand's digital media page replies with satisfaction that the complaint has been resolved and his problems are rectified.

For a brand manager who is testing waters in a regional market, customer conversations are like a live time bomb; it is a great opportunity to win customers' loyalty, but at the same time, one misstep also would result in losing a customer. The conversations, thus, must be well crafted and well planned to hit the right chords with the regional customer.

For example, the Indian Railways is very active on Twitter, constantly looking for customer complaints and queries. One such incident was when an 18-month baby was traveling by train in Uttar Pradesh and required milk, but all the pantries were closed. The baby's relative tweeted at the Indian Railways about it with details regarding the train. The request was escalated, and arrangements were made swiftly before the train reached the next station. The family was contacted and informed about the arrangements, and the milk was delivered to the family as promised at the next station.

This act of the Indian Railways won a great deal of positive image for them, and a lot of Twitter users were impressed. This kind of swift action and social media listening can help brands build companionship and confidence with the customers that they can come to you for any support or assistance.

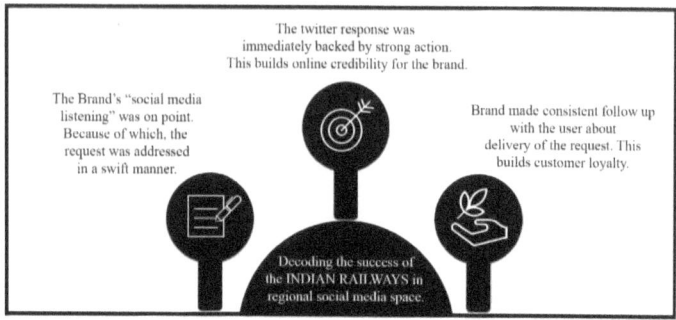

So, we have come to the end of the chapter. The takeaway from this chapter is key points on how to build a bond with the user.

Figure: How to build a bond with the regional user.

3.5. HOBBY

User-generated content (UGC) is soon becoming a commonly used "term" in the digital media ecosystem. What is user-generated content (UGC)? It is the content that is created by customers for the brand. The creation of content by users can range from answering contest questions, clicking selfies, to making videos for the brand, performing for the brand content like singing, dancing, acting. So, why is UGC becoming an integral part of the digital content strategy these days? Because they give fans an opportunity to turn from a passive receiver of content to an active creator of content.

Who does not like to be involved and recognized by a brand for their activities? There are various statistics and data collected by surveys that prove UGC impacts customer decisions vastly. To quote a few, according to Tintup, almost 90 percent of customers believe user-generated content like reviews and blogs impact their purchasing decisions. Even brands have seen 28 percent more engagement in campaigns involving UGC than other campaigns. These numbers are just the tip of the iceberg. It is common sense to note that when communication is two way, the impact it generates is higher.

It shows that the brand listens to the customer and provides a platform for the customers to show off their talents. This phenomenon is even higher in tier 2, 3 cities, towns, and villages. Because the users here more often than not get a platform to show the world their talents. To quote an example, Momspresso.com, a leading user-generated content platform for women that enables them to express themselves through text, audio, and video content across 10 languages, recently revealed insights into the explosive growth of regional content in the country.

The platform revealed that currently, 65 percent of the content created is in regional languages and accounts for 85 percent of page views. It further observed the growth of regional content creators by 228 percent; whereas regional language page views grew by 180 percent over the last 12 months. It can be seen that regional users, especially women, are more interested in creating user-generated content. This is because regional users, especially women who are housewives, are deprived of any platform to showcase their skills or talents due to the prevailing cultural and societal stigma in the rural parts of the country. These are useful data for regional brand managers to create effective UGC campaigns to get users to participate in your brand campaigns.

In this chapter, we will be looking at the steps a regional brand manager should take to ensure the effective implementation of the UGC component in their campaign strategy. There are two such important aspects.

1. Participation – Involving user in the content creation process, so that the user engages with the campaign better and shares the content to their network.

2. Appraisal – Recognizing and gratifying an user for his participation, so that he gets a feeling of self-appraisal and importance.

(i) Participation

One major aspect which opened windows for brands to engage much better with the audience in the digital world is the ability to allow them to participate in conversations and co-create content with them during their campaigns. With outdoor campaigns like billboards, banners, print campaigns like ads, editorials, or even tv, radio advertisements, this kind of instant two-way communication for brands with their audience is difficult to execute. For many years, managers found it difficult to measure and understand whether their campaign was a hit or flop; did it deliver the message to the customer as it intended to, how did the customer receive it, what were their reactions? All these questions were very difficult to answer with certainty.

However, with digital media, participation from users can be received almost instantly in the form of comments, content, reviews, and feedbacks. And such participation helps in bringing the user closer to the brand and helps in developing a bond. This is a much-needed process when a brand enters a new regional market. Therefore, brand managers should enhance techniques to solicit as much participation as possible from the regional users during their campaigns.

Some common techniques are to open a section where users can send reviews, feedbacks, and opinions on making the product better. Brand managers can set up teams to connect to these personally and hear their feedback in person. Users value these interactions at a great level. Gratifications that may be small but personal—something like brand accessories or merchandise can be given to the users to acknowledge their participation. These inputs from regional customers help brands develop unique insights about the market, which are otherwise very difficult to gather.

Similarly, brands can involve regional users to co-create content for their campaigns. The brand may be new to the regional market, but the users are an integral part of the region. They know the culture, tone, and language of the region much more than anyone. Campaigns such as contests that invite the users to create content like photos, TikTok videos, dance videos, acting videos, singing audios can have immense potential in regional markets. The regional users want a big platform to showcase their talents, and the brands want to create effective content in the regional market which is true to the roots of the land. The synergy between the two needs is UGC content.

Let us look at an example to showcase what UGC activation can do to a brand. 'Velli malare', an old Tamil song from a not-so-popular movie, became a sensation on the internet due to user-generated content on TikTok. The song, which had a lackluster release and zero playbacks on TV channels and even radio stations, suddenly gained traction on TikTok, where users from tier 2, 3 cities started performing for the song, as the song and lyrics connected well with them. Because of more and more users from these markets performing their own TikTok versions, the song got one crore views on YouTube suddenly because people wanted to see the original version of the song. More than one lakh users created their own versions on TikTok.

The result of this: a song that had zero presence on TV, radio, or any other platform became an overhit viral because of user participation on a platform like TikTok. This is a good case study for brands to realize the potential of these user-generated content formats and platforms.

(ii) Appraisal

So, we now understand that two-way communication helps UGC campaigns do really well for the brands in the regional market. However, to maximize the full potential of the campaigns, we must dig deep into the major motivating factor that drives a user to spend time engaging and creating content for a brand campaign. If we deep dive into this customer behavior, we can infer that the need to get appraised and appreciated in front of others is the main reason why a user participates in such content creation.

If a brand manager effectively does this part right, the user becomes well connected to the brand and continues to engage with the same behavior over time. What are some of the methods a brand manager can employ to achieve this?

One method is to share and promote the user-made content on the official pages of the brand and give shout-outs and credits to the user. What excites a small-town regional user more than watching their content being posted on a brand's official page and receiving hundreds of comments for their performances? This kind of activity makes sure the user has a highly rewarding experience and pushes a user to become loyal toward the brand in digital media.

One more activity that can be related to this is to encourage users to share the links of their video to their friends and family as well as ask them to react to their performances on the brand page. This kind of campaign will make the user excited because their video would be uploaded on a brand's official page. Secondly, their family and friends can get involved in the exercise; more than anyone else's comments, users will be more excited to receive what their close ones would say about their content. This way, the brand not only reaches the user but also reaches their network and also gets their engagement to the posts.

Also, brands can come up with prize money, foreign trips, etc. which can act as added incentives for the best content, thereby encouraging users to create better content and increasing competitiveness among regional users. Such competitiveness brings out great content. For example, a YouTube singer called Dhinchak Pooja, who is known for creating her own comical versions of popular Hindi songs, was called as a participant on 'Bigg Boss' show. For a small content creator, it is a great recognition by a brand to make her a contestant on a national show hosted by Salman Khan. Such appraisals help more and more users create more content for the brand, hoping someday even they will also be recognized.

Another method could be to extend these content co-creation activities to other mediums. Brands can select some of the best content that they receive from the regional markets and take these videos outside digital media to other mediums such as outdoor advertisements, TV, cinema halls, etc. Involving commoners to endorse brand messages through their content and talent will be a very rewarding experience for both the brand as well as the user. These are some of the appraisal techniques a manager can employ to gratify a customer who creates content for them, thereby making them loyal brand advocates in regional markets.

So, we have come to the end of the chapter. Here is the takeaway of important points on how brand managers can keep users engaged with their content.

Figure: How to keep users engaged with brand content.

3.6. ESCAPE

One major motivation factor for people to use the internet and consume content that we have not discussed so far is escape motivation. Today, in our busy lives, we are all bugged with work, tension, family pressure, and various other commitments. Sometimes, reality can be so overwhelming. The internet acts as a medium of escape in such conditions. Users want to suspend themselves from reality, into an alternate universe where they can be free of their day-to-day stress and problems. Therefore, their internet consumption is heavily influenced by escape motivation.

There are many research studies and surveys which validate this argument. For instance, researchers Susanno, Phedra, and Murwani conducted a study in 2019 to understand the reason behind heavy internet consumption by users to watch content continuously. They concluded in their study that users do that to temporarily escape from their problems and worries, as it gives them an opportunity to escape to a different world. Similarly, researchers Starosta, Izydorczyk, and Lizyńczyk also conducted a study in 2019, to identify the major motivation behind users binge-watching content on the internet one after another. They also concluded in their study that escape motivation is the single biggest reason for this type of user behavior. This behavior acts as a tool for users to regulate their negative emotions and stay afloat!

Brands that want to do very well on digital media should factor in to serve this need of the user—the need to escape, the need to get switched off from reality. It is needless to point out that escape motivations cause a bigger impact on regional users while compared to users from metropolitan cities. The reason is the availability of various avenues such as malls, pubs, stadiums, etc. for the latter to escape from stress. But options are minimal for the regional users from tier 2, 3 cities, towns, and villages. Therefore, the internet serves as their last retreat for escaping! So, how can a brand manager capitalize on this situation and use this platform as an opportunity to connect the brand much better with regional users, with escape motivations?

In this chapter, we will be looking at the steps a regional brand manager should take to use digital media strategies to provide users an escape from reality. By providing escape motivation, the brand solidifies its relationship with the regional user. The effective capitalization of escape motivation can be done in two stages.

1. Immerse – Content strategy to make users involve and engage deeper with the brand's content.

2. Breakout – Campaigns involving over the top, larger than life content ideas that will make user temporarily suspend from his daily stress and worries.

(i) Immerse

As discussed above, one important motivation factor for an internet user is escaping from reality. As a brand manager, if we are able to stitch together campaigns that allow users to immerse their focus completely inside our content, then users would be motivated to visit our brand pages more often and engage with our content more. How do we enable it?

The first step is to create content that consumes the user, then letting the user consume it. Content that is created for the campaign must have so many layers of engagement levels and so many dimensions of user interactions. This kind of content inspires users to get immersed in the consumption process. For example, brands can conduct Instagram live videos where they can conduct quizzes related to their industry; users who answer the maximum number of questions would be gratified with a gift voucher. This way, the users can be engaged for a long amount of time with the brand and also can escape from reality to shift their focus toward winning the quiz. These contents can even be contests, online competitions, multiplayer games, puzzles, and web series.

The second step is to use technology usefully. Today, connecting audiences from across the world is very simple with technology. AR technology and multi-user video calls are all creative ways for users to be immersed in brand content. For example, brands can upload 360-degree YouTube videos in which the product can be hidden somewhere in the room. Users can move around the room using AR technology and find the product. This is one way of immersing users, with technology.

A recent phenomenon that worked in this model is the PUBG game. PUBG allowed multiple users from different parts of the world to get together in a play area, interact, communicate with each other, and try to win the game. PUBG was such a hit in India because, after their tiring day of work, users wanted to escape to an alternate universe where they can chill out for a while. Even though all brands cannot develop a PUBG game for their content strategy, they can take the spirit and flavor of such immersive user experiences and inject them into their campaigns.

For example, brands can use Skype calls to conduct simple tambola games during the weekend, and the winner can be gratified with a gift voucher. It's a simple concept, but for users, it's a window to escape from reality. These kinds of simple yet effective ideas that enable escapes will connect well with regional users. Brands can spin together content like these in their campaign calendars and allow users to engage with full rigor so that they can escape from their reality and become regular users of our brand content—because we give a platform for them to escape!

(ii) Break Out

Break out campaigns are very instrumental in satisfying the user's need to escape from reality. What are break out campaigns? Crazy, larger-than-life, one-off campaigns which are too good to be true. Campaigns which promise users elevated experiences that are rarely possible in real life. Recently, one application that became extremely popular among users was Dream 11, where users pick their cricket team before a match, and according to players' performances in the match, the user with the best team wins the jackpot. Even after knowing that the outcomes of the players' performances are not in their hands, and only one dream team will win after every match, why are people thronging to the application to form their dream teams before the match? What is the logic behind it?

It is their belief that someday their choices would prove right and their team would end up as the dream team for the day and they would win the jackpot; that would enable users to break out from their reality and escape.

The brand manager should note down the spirit and the logic behind campaigns like these and inject them into their campaign ideas. If we consider the regional audience, their major break out, larger-than-life factors can be jotted into two types. One is experience-driven, and the other is gift-driven.

Cricket and cinema are celebrated by the regional audience in a larger-than-life fashion. The users are smitten by the celebrities and the sportsmen so much because of their onscreen performances. These celebrities are rarely accessible to users in their reality. Maybe if the brand offers experiences to users where they can meet and greet celebrities or converse with them on Instagram live, that would be a once in a lifetime experience for them that they would never forget. A regional consumer would be kicked to participate in a campaign like that. Also, the recall value for such a campaign is very high. The regional consumer would keep sharing this story with his peer network to boast of the time he spent with a celebrity. And whenever this experience pops up, the brand which enabled this experience for him would be remembered fondly. That is a great way for a new brand to enter the hearts of a regional consumer.

For example, Star Sports' regional accounts such as Tamil, Telegu, Kannada created an interesting way to engage users during the COVID lockdown situation. They asked users to send videos of them playing cricket inside their house or on the terrace with plastic balls. Star Sports then used those videos to package it like international cricket, using sound effects and graphics. They made their top commentators do commentary for these user videos. For regional users who have limited exposure, this is an out of the world moment for them to see their videos being commentated by top commentators like an international match. This is a good example of coming up with campaigns that will give users out of the world experiences that they will remember fondly.

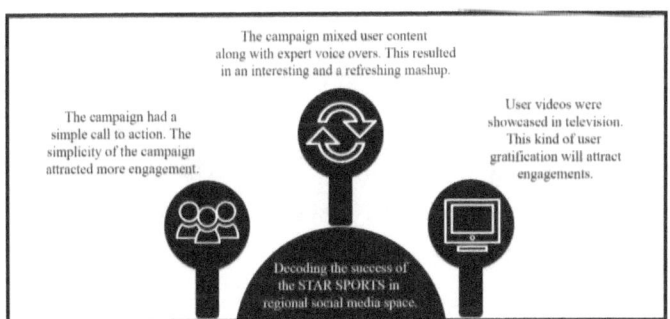

Similarly, if brands conduct brand contests and offer foreign trips to winners, it promises them experiences that could break them away from their reality. Also, brands can offer gifts such as accessories, gold coins, TVs, washing machines, grinders, mixers, etc. according to their target audience. Such mass gratifying campaigns create a mass emotion among users to participate in brand campaigns and stand a chance to win big prizes. That is the reason why campaigns like scratch and win, which announce prize money and gifts, do really well with customers.

For example, Udhayam Dal came out with a campaign called "Passport ilama foreign ah?" (Without a passport, travel to a foreign country) to attract tier 2, 3 city users. The campaign is about how Udhayam Dal will take care of the entire process of getting a passport, visa, tickets, and the entire documentation work for the winner, and then take them to a foreign country. For users from small towns, visa and passport are all terms that are intimidating; they fear the long documentation works that are required to go to foreign countries. Using this insight, Udhayam Dal came out with this campaign where winners of the contest need not worry about these documentation processes. Even users who do not have passports will stand a chance to go to a foreign country. This simple yet effective insight-based messaging clicked with the audience. The campaign was such a super hit, as it provided a break out experience for the target audience.

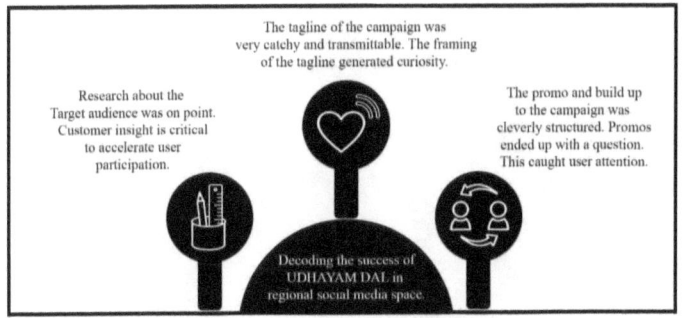

Users are constantly looking for opportunities and platforms that enable them to somehow escape from reality and transfer to an alternate world. Brand managers who are looking to launch their products successfully in regional markets can make use of this phenomenon to spread the word about their brands in the new market.

So, we have come to the end of the chapter. The takeaway from this chapter is a chart highlighting the methods that brands can use to construct various strategies to help users escape from reality.

Figure: How to get users to escape from reality with brand content.

CONCLUSION

With this, we have come to the end of the book. Through the book, we looked at various strategies that can help a brand manager sail through the journey of successfully launching their brands in regional markets. Through the three sections of the book, we touched upon the different touchpoints of the customer journey—from getting introduced to a new brand, to becoming a loyal customer of it through various digital media campaign techniques and strategies. Through the book, we have discovered how regional customers yearn for personalized, localized, vernacular content formats and pieces. We have laid down flowcharts and checklists as takeaways for brand managers to get the desired demand and respect for the brand from regional markets.

The first six chapters formed the first section of the book, where we discussed various plans and techniques a brand manager must employ to prepare the team for the challenges they would be facing in regional markets. We identified and highlighted the various expectations that regional users will have for the brands that enter their markets. We started the section with how brands must get the attention of regional users, with effective launch campaigns. We looked at strategies to change the user's attitude toward the brand, creating a positive outlook for the brand. We then looked at understanding and studying the regional user's beliefs through audits and past campaigns of competitors. We saw how by learning from the past, we can prepare a better content strategy, not make the same mistakes, and present an effective alternative to the existing players. We also looked at how brands can deliver quality content to introduce and communicate the positives as well as the various use cases of the brand's products in a better way to customers. Then we looked at two routes to winning a regional consumer's heart—information transfer and entertainment gratification.

The next six chapters formed the second section of the book, where we discussed various plans and techniques a brand manager must employ to effectively introduce new information relevant to the regional consumer and increment information on topics that regional consumers are already interested in. We looked at how the user's fear of missing out on information and updates can be catered to by the brands with content plans. We then analyzed the impact of social groups on the user's actions and how that can be utilized to create purchase intentions for users on social media. We looked at strategies to get the user to share/ forward the brand's content to their peer group networks using various techniques. We discussed various strategies to create relatable content for the regional user so that they can connect with the brand's content better. We looked at opportunities to present text content related to the brand in ways that will get users to binge-read and stay glued to it. We then found out methods to understand how users consume our content, and based on their behavior, suggest/ recommend suitable, personalized content for them to extract better reach and engagement in the regional market.

The final six chapters formed the third section of the book, where we discussed various plans and techniques a brand manager must employ to effectively engage the regional audience with entertainment content. We investigated how users develop parasocial bonds with onscreen characters and celebrities. We explored the ways brands can leverage those parasocial relationships through celebrity-led campaigns. We looked at how brands can study the preferences of regional users to create binge-worthy video content for brand campaigns. We investigated the need for companionship among internet users, how they value the internet as a virtual companion, and how brands can cater to that need by indulging in effective online conversations with the regional consumers. We then explored how brands can employ various strategies and techniques to make users constantly and consistently spend time consuming the brand's content. We also discussed how brands can provide memorable customer experiences for the users to escape from reality by devising "break out" campaigns.

Overall, with this book, we have made a modest attempt at guiding the reader to devise the perfect regional digital content strategy for their brands.

TESTIMONIALS

Arvin has put together an intensely practical guide that every Brand manager looking to enter a regional market should read. The book is full of actionable tips and techniques that will help a brand custodian understand the regional consumers and gain their attention through effective launch strategies that appeal to them. The book insists on the importance for brands to not just communicate in the regional language but also stay relevant and relatable to the regional consumers that will help a positive brand affiliation in the market. The book is well organized into 3 sections with flowcharts and checklists that will help the readers with key takeaways for achieving the desired results.

Arvin has taken regional strategies that have worked in the past with relevant examples and provides the tools, techniques and motivation to help every marketer understand the nuances of regional marketing and make it common practice.

– Abilasha Anish,
Senior Marketing Professional

This hand book is very relevant for digital marketers in today's context. When the internet is starting to penetrate into every Indian home, it is very critical for brands to speak and market in local languages with regional context in their digital media platforms. The methods and techniques discussed in this handbook will come in handy in such situations.

– Hitesh Rajwani,
CEO - Social Samosa

Today, technology has found a place in every aspect of doing business. This book by Arvin has been able to guide us with a plethora of examples and use-cases on framing the right digital strategy to tap the regional market. If you have a business and wish to make it digitally strong, this book is all you need.

– Seshu Karthick,
Founder & CEO - Dimensions Co